Understanding ADHD

I0127687

This essential guide provides accessible, concise, evidence-based guidelines on Attention Deficit Hyperactivity Disorder (ADHD), offering a deeper scientific understanding of the condition and its consequences. It offers ideas and insights for managing the condition in daily family life and promoting the most effective self-regulation strategies for children and adolescents, allowing parents to better understand the origins of their child's behaviour and avoid potential negative consequences.

In this straightforward text, Re and Capodieci set out the basic theories on ADHD and cover key topics including parent–child relationships, helping children understand their condition, friendships with peers, comorbidities, classroom strategies, and how families and professionals can best work together. Taking into account the most recent updates to the DSM-5 definition of ADHD, the authors emphasize the importance of a multifocal approach to the treatment of ADHD, involving the child's teachers, parents and peers, to better develop family and peer relationships. They offer strategies for the classroom, for good sleep and for healthy eating and physical activity, and support for any other learning, language, movement and emotional problems an ADHD child might have.

Understanding ADHD is essential reading for parents of children with ADHD, as well as health, education and social care professionals involved in the field.

Anna Maria Re is Associate Professor of Developmental and Educational Psychology, Department of Psychology, University of Turin, Italy.

Agnese Capodieci is a psychotherapist and researcher at the Department of General Psychology, University of Padova, Padova, Italy.

Understanding Atypical Development

Series editor: Alessandro Antonietti,
Università Cattolica del Sacro Cuore, Italy

This volume is one of a rapidly developing series in *Understanding Atypical Development*, published by Routledge. This book series is a set of basic, concise guides on various developmental disorders or issues of atypical development. The books are aimed at parents, but also professionals in health, education, social care and related fields, and are focused on providing insights into the aspects of the condition that can be troubling to children, and what can be done about it. Each volume is grounded in scientific theory but with an accessible writing style, making them ideal for a wide variety of audiences.

Each volume in the series is published in hardback, paperback and eBook formats. More information about the series is available on the official website at: www.routledge.com/Understanding-Atypical-Development/book-series/UATYPDEV, including details of all the titles published to date.

Published Titles

Understanding Tourette Syndrome
Carlotta Zanaboni Dina and Mauro Porta

Understanding Rett Syndrome
Rosa Angela Fabio, Tindara Caprì and Gabriella Martino

Understanding Conduct Disorder and Oppositional-Defiant Disorder
Laura Vanzin and Valentina Mauri

Understanding Giftedness
Maria Assunta Zanetti, Gianluca Gualdi and Michael Cascianelli

Understanding ADHD

A Guide to Symptoms, Management and Treatment

Anna Maria Re and
Agnese Capodieci

Routledge
Taylor & Francis Group

LONDON AND NEW YORK

First published 2020
by Routledge
2 Park Square, Milton Park, Abingdon, Oxon OX14 4RN

and by Routledge
52 Vanderbilt Avenue, New York, NY 10017

Routledge is an imprint of the Taylor & Francis Group, an informa business

© 2020 Anna Maria Re and Agnese Capodieci

The right of Anna Maria Re and Agnese Capodieci to be identified as authors of this work has been asserted by them in accordance with sections 77 and 78 of the Copyright, Designs and Patents Act 1988.

All rights reserved. No part of this book may be reprinted or reproduced or utilized in any form or by any electronic, mechanical, or other means, now known or hereafter invented, including photocopying and recording, or in any information storage or retrieval system, without permission in writing from the publishers.

Trademark notice: Product or corporate names may be trademarks or registered trademarks, and are used only for identification and explanation without intent to infringe.

British Library Cataloguing-in-Publication Data
A catalogue record for this book is available from the British Library

Library of Congress Cataloging-in-Publication Data
A catalog record has been requested for this book

ISBN: 978-0-367-19323-2 (hbk)
ISBN: 978-0-367-19324-9 (pbk)
ISBN: 978-0-429-20173-8 (ebk)

Typeset in Sabon
by Swales & Willis, Exeter, Devon, UK

Contents

Acknowledgements

We would like to thank Professor Cornoldi for his fundamental teaching, Professor Sorrentino and Dr Pavone for their precious suggestions and all the children, parents and teachers who contributed to making this book possible and who teach us something new every day.

Chapter 1

Signs and symptoms

Francis is an only child. He is ten years old and attending the last year of primary school. For some time now, his teachers have been insisting that his parents have him seen by a specialist because of his behaviour. From an early age, Francis was a difficult child to manage. He was always restless, and found it hard to adapt to regular sleeping and eating routines. At school he was very lively, but even when playing he would briefly pay attention to one game and then quickly move on to another. Even at home with his parents, his behaviour was no better. He would badger them incessantly for something, but often lose interest as soon as he had been granted what he wanted. His grandparents often accused his parents of being too indulgent with him and spoiling him. When he started primary school, the situation became worse. He had trouble staying seated at his desk, and was unable to concentrate during the lessons. He soon fell behind the rest of the class and his academic performance was generally poor. Getting his homework done was by no means easy. Francis would constantly postpone getting started, then do his homework all in a rush, making numerous mistakes. Sometimes he did not finish his homework because he had not written in his diary everything he was supposed to do, and sometimes he did none because he had not written anything at all. He often received notes from his school teachers or was punished at home for not doing his homework or for not trying hard enough. For Francis, life with his classmates was not easy either. He was often excluded from their games because he would keep wanting to dictate the rules, or he would want to play another game because he quickly became bored with one activity and wanted to move on to another. In an effort to make himself popular with his companions, he would often be the "class jester", telling jokes even when the teacher was explaining something, or poking fun at a classmate who was struggling. The teachers complained not only about Francis's behaviour, but also about his erratic academic performance. Sometimes he succeeded in completing a task with excellent results, and other times he refused even to try. This attitude gave his teachers the impression that Francis was "lazy", "poorly motivated" and "spoilt by his parents".

Introduction

The above description is typical of the picture of children with Attention Deficit Hyperactivity Disorder (ADHD) painted by their parents during their first meeting with a psychologist. "Charles can't sit still, not even for a minute", "Miki never succeeds in finishing anything he starts. He has hundreds of ideas but never follows any of them through", "Claude is always running around and climbing all over the place", "Francis never thinks about the consequences. He speaks and acts without thinking twice". These are the sort of comments that parents of children with ADHD often hear.

The reason why this disorder has such a long name (and one that is also rather daunting for a parent) is because it is characterized by its symptoms: inattention, hyperactivity and impulsivity.

Let us take a closer look at what is meant by each of these aspects.

The term *attention deficit* is used mainly to describe a difficulty in keeping focused on something for a prolonged period of time, especially when this demands a degree of intellectual effort. This difficulty is often revealed by a tendency to change the subject, a lack of perseverance and disorganization. It is not caused by an oppositional attitude or inability to understand what is required. Being easily distracted is another very common sign of attention deficit. In describing how difficult he found it to stay concentrated on listening to the teacher's explanation, a child once told me: "I really want to pay attention, but then if a pencil drops, or a fly goes by, I just can't keep my eyes on the teacher". His words give us a clue to how difficult it can be for a child with ADHD to stay focused, however hard they try. To better explain how our attention functions, we can imagine a net with holes in it that may be large or small, depending on what material we want to allow through. When the net has large holes, lots of material can pass through, but if we only want to let a little material through – in other words, when we want to select what we allow through the net – then we narrow the holes so that all the larger material remains outside. Our attention works in much the same way. When we are relaxing and going for a stroll, for instance, we are not paying attention to anything in particular. We allow our attention to wander from one thing (such as a shop window) to another (such as a passer-by). In other words, we allow the stimuli around us to briefly capture our attention. But when we are concentrating on something (when we are reading a book, for instance), then our attention focuses only on what we are reading and we are barely aware of all the stimuli around us (such as background noise). Children with ADHD struggle to narrow the holes in their "attention net", and are consequently easily distracted by the many stimuli in their surrounding environment (see Box 1.1). Many parents might be thinking that their children succeed in remaining concentrated for quite a while, oblivious to anything around them, when they are amusing themselves playing video games, for instance. This stems from the fact that motivation is a very important factor that can strongly influence anyone's behaviour – and children with ADHD are no exception. Another very important factor that contributes to making video games particularly appealing to children generally lies in the immediate gratification they receive. Like some other games (such as certain puzzles), video games are characterized by various levels of difficulty. They are designed in such a way that

---

Box 1.1 How to prepare the study environment

To avoid children with ADHD being easily distracted, parents and teachers are advised to create an environment that is not too stimulating when the children have to cope with a demanding task, such as studying. *Suggestion*: Before getting down to work, make sure that only the materials indispensable for the task are on the desk, e.g. a book, a pencil and a rubber. All the other items that children usually have in their school bags can be distracting. There is no need for them to have a whole pencil case to hand; if they do, the temptation to play with the various colours and the other pens will be too strong and they will become inattentive.

every player, even a beginner, can find a level of difficulty on which they are successful. With success comes some form of gratification (such as a cumulative score), and this motivates players to continue the game, to keep practising in order to improve their performance and move on to the next level of difficulty. Simply put, players are always dealing with a level of difficulty that coincides with the "optimal challenge": not so easy that it becomes boring and success can be taken for granted (in which case players would lose interest), and not so difficult that it discourages them from going ahead. This makes players think "I can do it if I try" and gives them great satisfaction when they succeed. These are the ideal conditions for learning (Vygotsky, 1931), and if school work and homework could be presented in the same way, there would be no more demotivated students – but sadly this is virtually impossible!

Now let us look at the other symptoms that are usually seen in ADHD: hyperactivity and impulsivity. Symptoms of hyperactivity mainly affect physical movements, appearing as excessive and unfocused motor activity, especially at inappropriate times. Examples are fidgeting, drumming fingers on the table and chattering excessively (Marzocchi, Re, & Cornoldi, 2019). Hyperactive children are usually extremely lively, constantly running and climbing, and show little interest in calmer pastimes. Impulsivity, on the other hand, is defined as the inability to control one's behaviour (Barkley, 1998). It becomes manifest in extremely hurried actions that have to be taken instantly, often at high risk to the individual concerned. Impulsivity can express a desire for immediate compensation. It can take the form of invasive behaviour (e.g. constantly interrupting other people) or making important decisions without reflecting on the possible longer-term consequences. Impulsive children may answer impetuously before someone has finished asking them a question. They cannot wait for their turn in a game. They switch from one activity to another without completing what they had previously started. It is usually a child's difficulty with keeping still and controlling their behaviour when the circumstances require them to do so that is the most obvious sign of ADHD. It is therefore hardly surprising that, for a long time, specialists would speak not of ADHD, but of hyperkinetic disorder, because hyperactivity seemed to be the main feature of the condition.

So, if we imagine a six-year-old child with ADHD entering a primary school classroom for the first time and being asked, right from the start, to remain seated in their place and listen to the teacher or perform tasks that demand concentration and cognitive effort, how are they likely to react? Predictably enough, many children with ADHD try to run out of the classroom in their early days at school, and one of their teachers' primary goals is to keep these children in class for a whole school day. Hyperactivity and impulsivity are the aspects of ADHD most difficult for teachers to manage. Children with ADHD behave in certain ways – such as acting without thinking and failing to wait their turn in conversations and games – that also pose problems when they play with their peers. They often want to change the rules of a game, refuse to play by the rules or want to play a different game. These are all types of behaviour that, with time, can damage their relations with their classmates. Sometimes, caught up in the excitement of a game, children with ADHD may be unable to control their actions or predict the consequences of an action, so they may be too abrupt, cause an accident and even do serious harm to someone they were playing with. It is easy to imagine the negative fallout on their social life. It is important not to confuse the impulsive and sometimes clumsy behaviour of children with ADHD with a form of aggressiveness, however. They have no intention of hurting their playmates or seeking revenge for some action taken by other children. Nonetheless, despite their good intentions, the "accident-prone", troublesome behaviour of children with ADHD can make their social life complicated.

Another characteristic of children with ADHD is a tendency to prefer tasks or games that offer instant compensation (however modest), rather than those that might be more rewarding but involve a greater commitment in terms of time and effort. This would explain why these children struggle to find their own inner motivation to engage in activities that are more demanding and take longer to complete (Sonuga-Barke, Taylor, & Heptinstall, 1992; Sonuga-Barke, Williams, & Hall, 1996). All these features become apparent in the spontaneous, sometimes violent, unfiltered way in which they express their emotions too. That is why children with ADHD are often considered rude and insensitive, and this adds to their problems when it comes to establishing mature and durable relationships.

Characteristics of ADHD

It is easy to imagine that many people can see the features we have just described in themselves, or are thinking of various other people, adults or children, who have trouble keeping focused on a job or act impulsively. In fact, many of us have these traits, though in most cases we do not have them all the time, but maybe only when we are more tired or stressed, and such behaviour is usually not obvious enough to have a negative effect on our daily lives. It is no accident that the main diagnostic manuals (Diagnostic and Statistical Manual of Mental Disorders, DSM, and International Classification of Diseases, ICD) always add the consideration: "There is clear evidence that the symptoms interfere with, or reduce the quality of, social, academic, or occupational functioning" (Symptoms and diagnostic criteria according to the DSM-5, APA, 2013), which represents one of the crucial criteria enabling a diagnosis to be established. Inattention, hyperactivity and impulsivity can all be seen as traits distributed along a continuum with an absence of the trait (e.g. no attention deficit) at one end and its constant presence (a continuous attention deficit) at the other. We all occupy a space somewhere along this continuum and it is only when we exceed a threshold such that our attention difficulties interfere with our daily lives that we can speak of symptoms and not just personality traits.

Although we might be inclined to think that ADHD is a very common disorder, major epidemiological studies and the main diagnostic manuals indicate that it affects from 3% to 5% of the school-age population. This percentage may not seem much to worry about, but it means that nearly one child in every 20 has the disorder. ADHD is more likely to affect boys than girls (the ratio is three to one). The reasons for this gender disparity are still not known, but any hyperactive behaviour is probably more obvious in boys, making those with ADHD easier to identify. Inattention may be the prevailing feature in girls, whose hyperactivity could be less evident. In fact, some authors believe that the disorder is likely to be underestimated in girls, and this would partly explain why the condition appears to have a male predominance.

In fact, ADHD can develop differently in different children. In the majority of cases children have symptoms of both attention deficit and hyperactivity to much the same degree, but in some cases they may only show signs of inattention (in which case we speak of children with the predominantly inattentive subtype of ADHD), or only appear predominantly to be hyperactive and impulsive (in which case we speak of the hyperactive-impulsive subtype of ADHD).

Children with the predominantly inattentive subtype of ADHD have severe difficulties in focusing their attention on anything. They are often described as having their "head in the clouds". They are not disruptive in class – and that is why their behaviour often goes unreported – but they fail to keep up with the lessons and they fall behind in their school work, in class and at home. Their parents need to constantly remind them to do their homework and keep them focused on the task. These children are always the last to finish getting ready to go somewhere, or at mealtimes. They are usually assessed by a specialist because of their learning difficulties in all school subjects, which are due to the fact that they find it so hard to pay attention to the lessons. They are very easily distracted when they are studying, and often fail to complete their homework, either because they forget to write down what they were meant to do or because they run out of time. Their parents often describe them spending whole afternoons over their books and still not finishing the tasks they were set because they are continuously becoming distracted or stopping for some reason.

Children with the hyperactive-impulsive subtype of ADHD are extremely lively. They make a nuisance of themselves in the classroom but succeed nonetheless in following the lessons and completing their assigned tasks or activities. Teachers and parents very often complain that these children could do so much better but it is as if they were constantly "in a hurry". For them, doing well means getting the job done as soon as possible and finishing before anyone else. Such children are often reprimanded or punished (with a low mark, for instance) because if they had worked more calmly and paid more attention they would have been able to do so much better. In this subtype of ADHD, there may also be more evident signs of aggressive or oppositional behaviour and this makes the picture rather more complex.

Secondary aspects of ADHD

As already mentioned in the previous section, the core symptoms of ADHD can have repercussions on a child's daily life. The problems that children with this disorder are likely to experience mainly concern their relationships with family, peers and teachers. Because of their particular behavioural traits, these children are often in trouble, both at home and at school. It may be because they are slow to get ready to go out or the last to finish their lunch. They often behave in a manner that makes them seem immature. For instance, they may interrupt when a parent is speaking on the telephone or make a fuss about not wanting to go to bed. The same sort of thing happens at school as well, where they butt in when the teacher is explaining something, only to report an episode that has nothing to do with the lesson underway. With their head in the clouds, they are often unable to keep up with their classmates when it comes to following an explanation or completing a task. Teachers often describe situations where they and the rest of the class have moved on from a history lesson to a dictation but then they notice that the child with ADHD is still gazing at the history book on their desk, which may even be shut! There are plenty of other examples in this vein, but they all have one thing in common: they give us the impression that children with ADHD are "miles away", with their head and body always busy doing something else. Of course, this means that parents and teachers have to keep reminding these children to pay attention, sometimes even reprimanding them sharply – not so much because of the gravity of what they have (or have not) done, but because it is exasperating to have to keep badgering them. Comments like "it seems impossible that, despite my telling the child a thousand times, day in day out, he keeps making the same mistake" or "he seems to be making fun of me" or, worse still, "he seems to be doing it deliberately" are typical of parents or teachers describing children with ADHD (see Box 1.2).

Box 1.2 Advice on rebukes

Advice for parents: Being scolded too frequently about so many daily issues can induce children to shrug off what their parents say. At the same time, it can also undermine their self-confidence. In this situation, children may develop a sort of mental shield so that rebukes "go in one ear and out the other". That is why parents are advised to try and ignore the more minor episodes of misbehaviour, and concentrate on only scolding their child about the most important matters.

Unfortunately, the symptoms of ADHD negatively affect children's relationships with their peers too. These children are not usually seen as being good fun to play with. They can be bullies. They always want to dictate the rules of the game, to be the leader of a group, so they can be troublesome. In expressing their emotions, they may have a limited degree of self-control, so they sometimes exaggerate – both in their positive manifestations of joy and affection, and in their negative manifestations of anger, for instance. This can sometimes have important negative consequences, as in the case when they hurt a classmate or break something.

All these issues contribute to casting anyone with ADHD in a negative light. In childhood and adolescence, individuals with this disorder experience a strong need to be accepted and to establish relations with others, but they typically have weak social skills. There is evidence to suggest that they have a limited understanding of the implicit and explicit rules governing social behaviour and communication, and this prevents them from correctly interpreting non-verbal messages (e.g. body language). In addition, certain traits typical of ADHD – such as a limited tolerance of frustration (which often prompts what looks like wilful misbehaviour), impulsiveness, refusal to obey the rules, bullying, rapid mood swings, obstinacy, fits of anger and a lack of self-esteem – can all interfere with a child's ability to fit in, make friends, maintain satisfactory social relations and solve interpersonal conflicts (Kirby & Grimley, 1986).

If we try for a moment to put ourselves in their place, it is easy to see that being constantly reprimanded by their teachers or fighting with their parents cannot fail to have consequences for children with ADHD. One of the things that happens most frequently is that they tend to lose their self-esteem. Being constantly told they are not trying hard enough and seeing that they struggle with tasks that other children apparently find easy are situations that are bound to make children with ADHD feel inadequate. With time, as they accumulate negative experiences, they may even develop serious problems, such as anxiety or depression. This does not happen to all children with ADHD; nonetheless, it is essential to bear in mind that much of their inappropriate behaviour is not due to any lack of goodwill on their part but to a genuine disability. I once asked a child who had come for an assessment if he knew why he was there and he answered: "Because you're a teacher who can teach me how to be good".

I think this reflects the nature of children with ADHD: they would really like to do what is expected of them, but they cannot. It is up to the adults to help these children cope with their difficulties, see their efforts rewarded and become better integrated.

Comorbidities

Another characteristic of ADHD is that it is often associated with other disorders. In this case, we speak of comorbidities, meaning the simultaneous presence of two or more separate disorders. In the case of ADHD, this is unfortunately quite a common situation, affecting approximately one in every two cases (Guidetti & Galli, 2006). The disorders most commonly associated with ADHD are of a behavioural type (Jensen, Martin, & Cantwell, 1997), such as oppositional defiant disorder or conduct disorder. Comorbidity with a learning disability (LD) is also a very frequent finding (DuPaul, Gormley, & Laracy, 2013). These comorbidities contribute to making life difficult for children with ADHD, particularly at school. In fact, one of the main negative consequences of ADHD concerns how it affects children's academic performance – whether they have a known comorbid learning disabilities or not. In some cases, there may be a genuine concomitance of two distinct problems (e.g. dyslexia and ADHD). In others, even without any apparent comorbidities, the loss of motivation or low self-esteem experienced by children with ADHD can often contribute to impairing their academic achievements. In yet other cases, a typical characteristic of ADHD – such as a difficulty controlling irrelevant information or planning – can produce symptoms both of ADHD and of learning disabilities, especially in complex tasks such as mathematical problem-solving (Marzocchi, Lucangeli, De Meo, Fini, & Cornoldi, 2002; Re, Lovero, Cornoldi, & Passolunghi, 2016) or expressive writing (Re, Caeran, & Cornoldi, 2008; Re, Pedron, & Cornoldi, 2007). To give an instance, Marzocchi et al. (2002) studied the influence of irrelevant information on mathematical problem-solving, comparing children with ADHD with typically developing, control children. They found that children with ADHD performed just as well as controls in problems that only contained relevant information, but the former's performance was far worse than the latter's in problems that also contained irrelevant information. The outcome was the same regardless of whether the irrelevant information was included at the start or at the end of the text, and whether it was of verbal or numerical type. A possible explanation for these results lies in the fact that children with ADHD have difficulty distinguishing between what is relevant and what is not. An excessive amount of information overloads their minds (and their memory in particular), preventing them from finding the most appropriate approach to solving a problem.

In a similar study, Re et al. (2008) investigated how children with ADHD could be helped to improve their performance in written compositions. The children were asked to write a letter in two different conditions: in one, they were given no guidance; in the other, they were given an outline to follow. The purpose of the outline was to divide the writing process into a set of steps to help the children plan what they wanted to say, since it is clear from the literature that children with ADHD have weak planning skills (see Chapter 2). The results of the study demonstrated that children with ADHD performed better in various aspects of the writing task when given an outline to follow and especially in terms of their spelling (they made far fewer spelling mistakes). The authors concluded that, faced with such a complex task as spontaneous writing can be, children with ADHD did not have enough resources to concentrate on their spelling, so they made numerous mistakes. But if they were given help with one of the aspects of spontaneous writing that children with ADHD find more difficult – i.e. planning what to say – this left more attention resources available to spend on their spelling so they made fewer mistakes.

It is therefore always very important to monitor the academic performance of children with ADHD and to maintain an ongoing exchange with teachers to avoid the problems typical of this disorder becoming more severe and worsening the child's school life.

Developmental aspects

Although ADHD is a disorder that frequently becomes apparent in early childhood, there is increasing scientific and clinical evidence that the disorder persists throughout an individual's life (SINPIA, 2002). In fact, longitudinal studies have identified various symptoms of ADHD in adolescence and adulthood as well (e.g. Jensen, 2009; Klein & Mannuzza, 1991; Mannuzza & Klein, 2000). But, as children grow up and change, so too do the signs and symptoms of the disorder. Generally speaking, what happens is that the most visible exterior manifestations – such as motor hyperactivity – diminish with time, making the child easier to manage. The more cognitive aspects – such as inattention and poor planning skills – tend instead to persist. That is why intervention for children who have ADHD is usually provided at various times in their lives and especially at the most crucial stages of their development, such as the passage from childhood to adolescence.

The most severe symptoms of motor hyperactivity are seen in early childhood. For instance, while playing, a child may tire easily of one game and be constantly in search of other games and new stimuli. Such children are unlikely to concentrate on and complete any given activity, even if it is a game. That said, when signs of inattention and hyperactivity are apparent already in early childhood, it is very difficult to say for sure whether they are simply an indication of liveliness or symptoms of a disorder like ADHD. As Sonuga-Barke and colleagues pointed out (Sonuga-Barke, Auerbach, Daley, & Thompson, 2005), there are plenty of children under five years old who show high levels of motor activity but do not develop a genuine behavioural disorder. Another problem concerns the paucity of tools for assessing ADHD in preschool age (Re & Cornoldi, 2009). In short, we always need to be very cautious about establishing a diagnosis of ADHD in children under six or seven years old.

The times when ADHD seems to be most evident and pose more problems coincide with the passage from one type of school to the next, because the environmental demands increase. For instance, when children start primary school they have to start learning to cope with increasingly complex tasks and new social rules. Then, when they move up to secondary school, they need to learn to study more on their own.

It is usually at the start of their school careers that the problems encountered by children with ADHD first become fully apparent. This is probably because these children struggle to meet the demands of their new environment and school drastically reduces their opportunities for play, and especially their freedom of movement.

With primary school, the children's difficulties increase because there are more rules to comply with and more tasks to complete. Teachers continue to describe children with ADHD as "immature" by comparison with their peers, especially from the behavioural standpoint, but we know that this apparent immaturity stems largely from the core characteristics of the disorder. During their years at primary school, children with ADHD continue to be very active and, although they are just as intelligent as their classmates, their behaviour seems immature for their chronological age and they may begin to show signs of learning disabilities. Their attention deficit leads to major problems with planning and organizing their school work and coordinating their activities; this may increasingly obstruct the academic progress of children with ADHD as they grow up (Cantwell, 1996). For instance, Barkley, Fischer, Smallish and Fletcher (2006) found that the likelihood of them having to repeat a year at school was at least eight times higher than average.

The behavioural issues of children with ADHD appear more or less severe depending on the situation. When they are free to play at whatever they like and have ample opportunity for movement, they do not seem to have any particular problems. But in settings where they need to comply with rules, they are described as "troublesome" or "unmanageable". Their difficulties with interpersonal relationships, often already evident in preschool age, tend to persist and become worse as they grow older. This is probably because an appropriate interaction with their peers demands more and more social and communicational expertise and self-control. Meanwhile, outward signs of hyperactivity tend to diminish in terms of frequency and intensity as they grow up and may be partially replaced by an "interiorized agitation", which can be expressed as intolerance, impatience, switching constantly from one activity to another or fidgeting (Fischer, Barkley, Fletcher, & Smallish, 1993). As mentioned earlier, as children with ADHD grow older, they may develop behavioural traits that make it even more difficult for them to fit in socially. They can become obstinate, disobedient, overbearing and moody. They can find it hard to cope when their wishes are frustrated and have fits of anger; and they suffer from a lack of self-esteem. As they move on from childhood to adolescence, their uncontrollable behaviour and inattention interfere with their acquisition of indispensable social skills. In fact, teenagers with ADHD show a weak capacity to maintain their friendships and deal with conflictual interpersonal relationships (Kirby & Grimley, 1986).

With adolescence comes other, bigger problems for individuals with ADHD. The typical emotional difficulties associated with this developmental stage can be exacerbated by the disorder, leading to genuine episodes of depression and anxiety, and a further loss of self-esteem. This situation is aggravated by the fact that these youngsters have often already had various negative experiences, especially in their social relations with their peers (Re, Pedron, & Lucangeli, 2010). While there is usually evidence of a slight improvement in the typical symptoms of ADHD, their problems are by no means over. In a follow-up study on adolescents diagnosed with ADHD during their primary school years, Lambert (1988) found that approximately three in every four of them still showed signs of the disorder. The problems relating to personal identity, peer acceptance and physical development that are typical of adolescence cannot always be managed successfully by teenagers with ADHD. Their unavoidable difficulties in these developmental milestones can add to any existing problems of low self-esteem, lack of self-confidence and even clinically significant anxiety and depression (Barkley, Fischer, Edelbrock, & Smallish, 1990).

ADHD also persists into adult age, when the related symptoms of hyperactivity and impulsivity fade further, but attentional and planning difficulties remain. For instance, adults with ADHD may frequently forget studying or occupational commitments. They can have difficulty predicting future events. They may have an impulsive personality, or even an antisocial personality disorder. They may encounter marital problems, mismanage their finances, engage in illicit activities or keep changing their jobs. In other words, the disorder continues to pose social and occupational problems even in adulthood. It is also often associated with comorbidities, cigarette smoking and substance abuse (Wilens & Dodson, 2004). As concerns the proportion of adults with ADHD, a meta-analysis conducted by Faraone and colleagues (Faraone, Biederman, & Mick, 2006) concluded that the "full" disorder persists into adulthood only in approximately 15% of the population diagnosed with ADHD in their childhood. But approximately 65% of the adults still affected continue to have some symptoms of the disorder that interfere with their social and occupational life.

All this should not discourage parents, because all the troublesome issues associated with ADHD can have positive as well as negative outcomes. The important thing for parents of children with this disorder is to help them throughout their lives to deal in the best possible way with the difficulties they encounter. Of course, it is impossible to protect them from everything that may happen, but this applies to all other children as well.

References

American Psychiatric Association. (2013). *Diagnostic and statistical manual of mental disorders* (5th ed.). Washington, DC: Author.

Barkley, R. A. (1998). *Attention-deficit hyperactivity disorder: A handbook for diagnosis and treatment* (2nd ed.). New York: Guilford Press.

Barkley, R. A., Fischer, M., Edelbrock, C. S., & Smallish, L. (1990). The adolescent outcome of hyperactive children diagnosed by research criteria: I. An 8-year prospective follow-up study. *Journal of the American Academy of Child and Adolescent Psychiatry, 29,* 546–557.

Barkley, R. A., Fischer, M., Smallish, L., & Fletcher, K. (2006). Young adult outcome of hyperactive children: Adaptive functioning in major life activities. *Journal of the American Academy of Child and Adolescent Psychiatry, 45*(2), 192–202.

Cantwell, D. P. (1996). Attention deficit disorder: A review of the past 10 years. *Journal of the American Academy of Child and Adolescent Psychiatry, 35,* 978–987.

DuPaul, G. J., Gormley, M. J., & Laracy, S. D. (2013). Comorbidity of LD and ADHD: Implication of DSM-5 for assessment and treatment. *Journal of Learning Disabilities, 46*(1), 43–51.

Faraone, S. V., Biederman, J., & Mick, E. (2006). The age-dependent decline of attention deficit hyperactivity disorder: A meta-analysis of follow-up studies. *Psychological Medicine, 36*(2), 159–165.

Fischer, M., Barkley, R., Fletcher, K., & Smallish, L. (1993). The stability of dimensions of behaviour in ADHD and normal children over an 8-year follow-up. *Journal of Abnormal Child Psychology, 21,* 315–337.

Guidetti, V., & Galli, F. (2006). *Neuropsichiatria dell'infanzia e dell'adolescenza [Child and adolescent neuropsychiatry].* Bologna, Italy: Il Mulino.

Jensen, P. S. (2009). Clinical considerations for the diagnosis and treatment of ADHD in the managed care setting. *The American Journal of Managed Care, 15*(5), S129–S140.

Jensen, P. S., Martin, D., B.A., & Cantwell, D. P. (1997). Comorbidity in ADHD: Implications for research, practice, and DSM.V. *Journal of the American Academy of Child & Adolescent Psychiatry, 36*(8), 1065–1079.

Kirby, E. A., & Grimley, L. K. (1986). *Disturbi dell'attenzione e iperattività: Guida per Psicologi e Insegnanti [Attention and hyperactivity disorders: Guide for Psychologists and Teachers].* Trento, Italy: Erickson.

Klein, R. G., & Mannuzza, S. (1991). Long-term outcome of hyperactive children: A review. *Journal of the American Academy of Child and Adolescent Psychiatry*, *30*(3), 385–387.

Lambert, N. M. (1988). Adolescent outcome for hyperactive children. *American Psychologist*, *43*, 786–799.

Mannuzza, S., & Klein, R. G. (2000). Long-term prognosis of attention-deficit/hyperactivity disorder. *Child and Adolescent Psychiatric Clinics of North America*, *9*(3), 711–726.

Marzocchi, G. M., Lucangeli, D., De Meo, T., Fini, F., & Cornoldi, C. (2002). The disturbing effect of irrelevant information on arithmetic problem solving in inattentive children. *Developmental Neuropsychology*, *21*, 73–79.

Marzocchi, G. M., Re, A. M., & Cornoldi, C. (2019). Disturbo di Attenzione/Iperattività. In C. Cornoldi (a cura di), *Difficoltà e Disturbi dell'Apprendimento [Learning difficulties and Learning Disabilities]* (pp. 301–331). Bologna, Italy: Il Mulino.

Re, A. M., Caeran, M., & Cornoldi, C. (2008). Improving expressive writing skills of children rated for ADHD symptoms. *Journal of Learning Disabilities*, *41*(6), 535–544.

Re, A. M., & Cornoldi, C. (2009). Two new rating scales for assessment of ADHD symptoms in Italian preschool children. *Journal of Attention Disorders*, *12*, 532–539.

Re, A. M., Lovero, F., Cornoldi, C., & Passolunghi, M. C. (2016). Difficulties of children with ADHD symptoms in solving mathematical problems when information must be updated. *Research in Developmental Disabilities*, *59*, 186–193.

Re, A. M., Pedron, M., & Cornoldi, C. (2007). Expressive writing difficulties in children described as exhibiting ADHD symptoms. *Journal of Learning Disabilities*, *40*(3), 244–255.

Re, A. M., Pedron, M., & Lucangeli, D. (2010). *ADHD e Learning Disabilities. Metodi e strumento di intervento [Methods and intervention tool]*. Milano, Italy: Franco Angeli.

SINPIA (2002). *Linee guida per la diagnosi e la terapia farmacologica del Disturbo da Deficit Attentivo con Iperattività (ADHD) in età evolutiva.* [Guidelines for the diagnosis and the pharmacological treatment of ADHD], www.sinpia.eu/atom/allegato/149.pdf.

Sonuga-Barke, E. J., Auerbach, J., Campbell, S. B., Daley, D., & Thompson, M. (2005). Varieties of preschool hyperactivity: Multiple pathways from risk to disorder. *Developmental Science*, *8*, 141–150.

Sonuga-Barke, E. J. S., Taylor, E., & Heptinstall, E. (1992). Hyperactivity and delay aversion II: The effect of self versus externally imposed stimulus presentation periods on memory. *British Journal of Developmental Psychology*, *33*(2), 399–409.

Sonuga-Barke, E. J. S., Williams, E., Hall, M., & Saxton, T. (1996). Hyperactivity and delay aversion III: The effect on cognitive style of imposing delay after errors. *Journal of Child Psychology and Psychiatry, 37*(2), 189–194.

Vygotsky, L. S. (1931). *Mind in society.* Cambridge, MA: Harvard University Press.

Wilens, T. E., & Dodson, W. (2004). A clinical perspective of Attention-Deficit/Hyperactivity Disorder into adulthood. *The Journal of Clinical Psychiatry, 65*(10), 1301–1313.

Chapter 2

What causes ADHD?

Theories and perspectives

Introduction

For people who know nothing about ADHD, the behaviour of children with this disorder may seem merely the outcome of a poor upbringing. Their parents are often told that these children behave as they do "because they're spoilt"; or people may even say: "Leave them with me for a week and they'll soon stop all this misbehaving!". In actual fact, it is hard to explain and deal with the troublesome behaviour of children with ADHD. To find ways to "solve" their issues or cope with certain types of behaviour it is important to try and understand what causes them.

But finding the cause of ADHD is no easy matter. Numerous attempts have been made to explain the nature of this disorder and various scientific disciplines have been involved in researching it. Here we review the main theoretical explanations for the condition and the most significant studies conducted on the topic.

The neuroscientific approach

First of all, we need to stress that the origins of the disorder are neurobiological. Even though upbringing and the environment have a fundamental role in a child's development, they are not enough to explain why some children develop ADHD. In actual fact, the real cause of the disorder has still not been identified, but various factors are known to contribute to the risk of its onset.

In recent decades, ADHD has become one of the most often studied childhood syndromes, discussed the world over (Marzocchi, Re, & Cornoldi, 2019) by scholars in various disciplines. Psychologists, neuroscientists and geneticists have all added to what we know about this complex and multifaceted disorder. Below we review the most significant studies and the latest results of scientific research on ADHD.

There are risk factors that we could describe as biological, consisting in conditions that influence children's physical development, which may depend on their genetic heritage or on adverse factors that occurred during a mother's pregnancy or immediately after a child's birth. Among the latter factors, the most predictive seem to be the mother's use of alcohol or cigarette smoking in pregnancy, and a low birthweight in babies born prematurely. During pregnancy, cigarette smoke exposes the foetus to the risk of absorbing nicotine, which can negatively affect the child's developing memory and raise the risk of ADHD. The mother's use (and especially abuse) of alcohol during pregnancy is equally risky. The various risks to which such behaviour exposes their children include an approximately 2.5-fold higher than average risk of developing ADHD. A low body weight at birth associated with prematurity also exposes children to a higher risk of ADHD; this is because the newborn's weight is usually a good indication of the child's overall development.

Numerous studies have tried to find a "genetic cause", i.e. a gene responsible for the onset of ADHD. Two types of research have been conducted to identify the gene involved: population genetics and molecular genetics.

The most important studies of the first type have investigated interactions between genes and the environment. This involves studying family members, homo- and heterozygote twins (homozygote twins have exactly the same genetic heritage, while heterozygote twins have only a part of their genes in common, like any two siblings) and adopted children. Such studies have shown that there is a familial element to the disorder. For instance, if either parent has ADHD, it is more likely that one of their offspring will have the disorder too. Of course, this phenomenon is not only due to genetics, since the children also share the environment in which they live with their parents. When children show some problematic behavioural traits, it is highly likely that they will have experienced them at home and assimilated them in the repertoire of their own behaviour. Nonetheless, a recent study (Faraone & Larsson, 2018) reviewed 37 genetic population studies conducted on twins, and the authors found evidence of the heritability of symptoms of ADHD in 74% of cases on average. This means that biological causes of genetic type account for a sizable proportion of the children affected, but genetic causes cannot explain the origin of the disorder in 100% of cases. A good deal of the reasons for the phenomenon still come down to environmental factors; proof of this lies in the fact that interventions undertaken with parents, schools and the children themselves can achieve important improvements in the life of children with ADHD.

Research in molecular genetics seeks to identify one or more specific genes responsible for the disorder. For the time being, no single gene has been pinpointed as the cause of ADHD. In all likelihood, it is a polygenic disorder. In other words, it stems from the combined effects of several genes and their effects are modulated (amplified or reduced) by environmental factors. Most of the molecular genetic studies conducted to date have identified several genes responsible for regulating the presence of dopamine in the brain (such as DAT1, DRD4, DRD5). Dopamine is a neurotransmitter, i.e. a substance naturally present in everyone's brain that is needed to enable our brain cells, or neurons, to communicate with one another. Neurons are special in that they communicate with one another thanks to their extremities, which contain receptors for the neurotransmitters. Our brain works by means of countless continuous, rapid communications. Neurotransmitters have a very important role in ensuring proper brain functioning. We have seen from various studies, and also in clinical practice (for instance, from the effects of drugs such as methylphenidate, which we discuss in Chapter 4), that children with ADHD have lower than normal levels of dopamine in their brain's intersynaptic spaces (the gaps between one neuron and the next). This could be due either to an excessive reuptake of dopamine or to the receptors working too hard.

The neurosciences are a branch of study that spans psychology and neurology and is interested in identifying the anatomical substrate related to the behavioural manifestations of a disorder (which is the brain, in the case of ADHD). In recent years, new technologies have enabled us to considerably improve our neuroscientific knowledge of the disorder. These technologies mainly involve magnetic resonance imaging (which provides a "photograph" of the brain's structure) and functional magnetic resonance (showing us which areas of the brain are activated when we do certain things). We have recently also begun to use a technique called diffusion tensor imaging, which enables us to "see" the connections between neuron circuits by analysing the water molecules contained in the brain. Research efforts to reveal the features peculiar to the brain of a child with ADHD have mainly compared samples of children with and without the disorder. Numerous studies have consistently concluded that the circuit most affected in ADHD extends from the prefrontal regions to the striated body and as far as the cerebellum. This lengthy circuit points to an involvement of the cognitive (frontal) and emotional (striated body) processes, and those regulating various motor, language and time-estimating mechanisms, among others (cerebellum).

Neurocognitive models

While the neuroscientists have been busy, other researchers have considered whether ADHD might have a cognitive basis. In other words, they have tried to explain the disorder on the grounds of the cognitive processes that are impaired in the children affected. In the 1990s, numerous studies identified ADHD-related problems in various executive functions, an "umbrella" term used to indicate higher-order cognitive processes such as planning, working memory and inhibition. One of the most popular theories circulating in the 1990s was developed in the USA by Russel Barkley, who published an article describing his theoretical model in 1997 (Figure 2.1).

According to Barkley, ADHD is caused essentially by an inhibition problem that gives rise to difficulties with working memory, emotional self-control, motivation and arousal (the meaning of which is explained in the next paragraph), the interiorization of speech, and the analysis and synthesis of events (reconstitution). To give an example, if children have difficulty inhibiting irrelevant information in their working memory, their mind becomes overcrowded with information and this makes it difficult for them to stay focused on an explanation or complete a task. In the same way, if they find it hard to control their emotions, their behaviour may become disruptive and sometimes impulsive, with negative consequences that the children themselves may regret.

Meanwhile, in Europe, Sergeant and his colleagues (Sergeant & Van der Meere, 1990; Sergeant, Van der Meere, & Oosterlaan, 1999) were developing their so-called cognitive-energetic model. This theoretical model envisages three levels: superordinate, energetic and information processing. The superordinate level is concerned with coordinating actions and is the site of the executive functions.

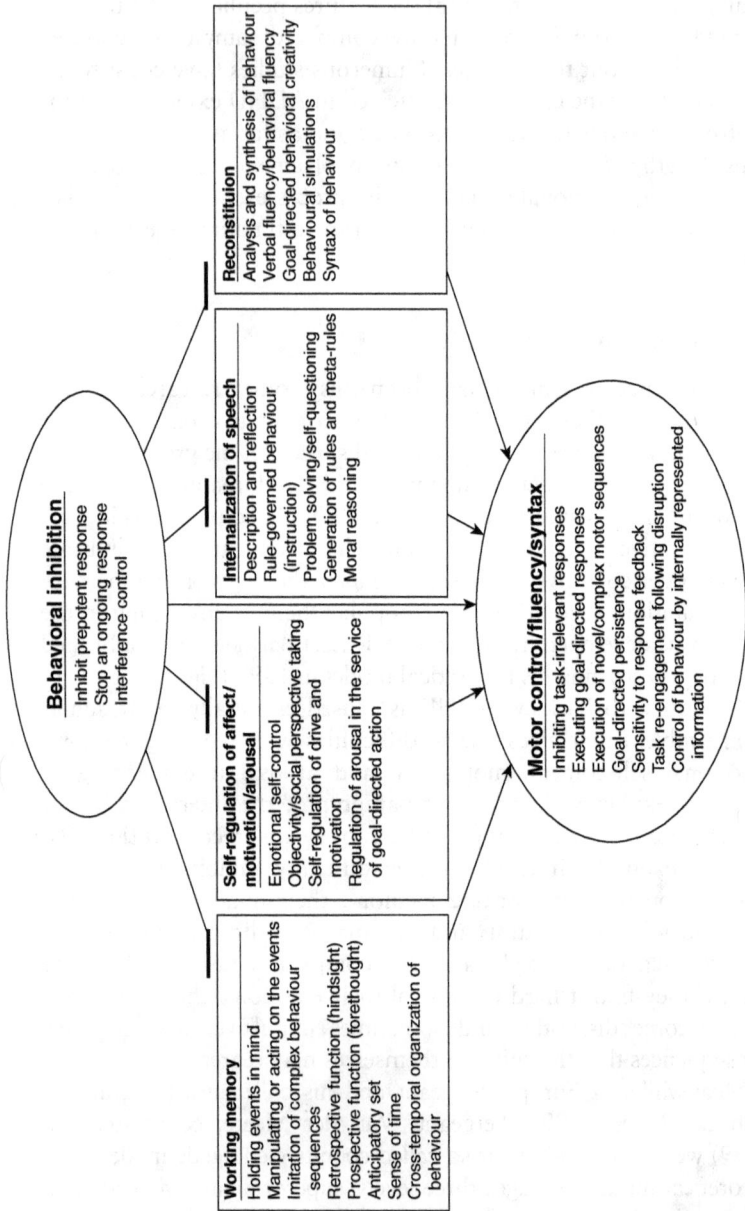

Figure 2.1 Barkley's theoretical model (1997)

The second level is strictly energetic, involving three types of "resources". The first is effort (used to make available the energy needed to complete a task) and this controls the other two, which are arousal and activation. Arousal is defined as the energy needed to provide a rapid response (usually to analyse stimuli). Activation is the energy needed to remain vigilant. The third level, information processing, consists of three systems: encoding, processing and motor response. According to the model proposed by Sergeant and colleagues (Sergeant & Van der Meere, 1990; Sergeant et al., 1999), children with ADHD have a weak activation component and this gives rise to an impaired motor response, while their arousal-encoding circuit remains intact. Sergeant concluded that children with ADHD have an impairment that affects the higher cognitive control component, i.e. their executive functioning.

Although these models have become milestones in research on ADHD, numerous other studies have attributed a more limited role to the executive functions. In particular, reports first from Pennington and colleagues, and later from Wilcutt and colleagues (Pennington & Ozonoff, 1996; Wilcutt, Doyle, Nigg, Faraone, & Pennington, 2005), showed that the executive functions cannot be the "core deficit" behind ADHD, as previous studies had often tried to demonstrate. There are various reasons why not, but two are particularly important: (i) not all children with ADHD have executive functions deficits; and (ii) not all children with ADHD reveal the same impairments in tasks that measure their executive functions. In other words, a task has yet to be identified – among all those used to test executive functions – in which all children with ADHD encounter difficulties. These children's performance in such tests can vary considerably. The above-mentioned authors thus concluded that executive functions are certainly an aspect in which children with ADHD are very often impaired, but we need to look further to find other factors that can contribute to explaining the disorder.

Other, more recently developed theoretical models have tried to combine and expand on earlier research in the light of the latest findings. An example is the theoretical model proposed by Castellanos and Tannock (2002): by pooling the genetic and environmental risk factors, they identified a number of endophenotypes that make a child more vulnerable to the onset of ADHD. Endophenotypes are quantifiable and genetically inheritable indicators of a greater likelihood of developing a given disorder or disease (in cardiology, for instance, a high blood-cholesterol level can be seen as an endo-phenotype associated with the risk of cardiovascular diseases). According to Castellanos and Tannock (2002), the endophenotypes for ADHD concern: (i) motor hyperactivity and the related neuro-biological connections with the dopaminergic system (and this would explain the efficacy of methylphenidate in controlling hyper-activity); (ii) an impaired inhibition of impulsive responses; (iii) a limited tolerance of having to wait (a trait emphasized in the Sonuga-Barke model described in the next paragraph); (iv) a deficient capacity for temporal analysis; and (v) a poor working memory. Castellanos and Tannock (2002) recommend using neu-roscientific methods to clarify the explanatory links between the various genetic, neurobiological, neuropsychological and symptom-based analyses on the causes of ADHD. They suggest starting from the genes that govern the regulation of a network of neurotransmit-ters, and going on to consider the cognitive mechanisms deriving from them and the clusters of symptoms (clinical subtypes) that depend on which specific cognitive competences are impaired.

Sonuga-Barke and colleagues (Sonuga-Barke, Bitsakou, & Thompson, 2010) subsequently attempted to integrate the neuro-anatomical, neurobiological and neuropsychological elements into a single model of ADHD, which envisages potential deficiencies in three circuits. The authors identified the neuropsychological factor corresponding to each of these circuits. As well as an impaired inhibition, which comes within the domain of the executive func-tions, controlled by a dorsal circuit, the authors suggest: a second ventral circuit governing motivation and, particularly, the inability to wait (*delay aversion*) and gratifications; and a third cerebellar motor circuit controlling children's capacity to synchronize their responses and their reaction times.

The first pathway is characterized by a particular weakness in inhibitory control, which mediates two effects on the developmental outcomes of children with ADHD: a lack of behavioural control and a significant limitation of their ability to engage in a task. Their lack of behavioural control mediates the onset of symptoms of ADHD, while their inability to engage in a task is sustained by cog-nitive dysfunctions. These cognitive impairments account for the classic pattern of difficulties that children with ADHD encounter in tasks that demand attentional flexibility, good planning and behav-ioural self-monitoring abilities, and an intact working memory. The second pathway is related to motivation and delay aversion. It is considered not as a core symptom, but as a characteristic that emerges later on, mediating the connection between behavioural symptoms, ability to engage in a task and a biologically altered reward mechanism. In this model, the link between ADHD symptoms and altered response mechanisms is mediated by a limited ability to wait, which becomes worse with the amount of time spent waiting. This shortened delay–reward gradient makes children with ADHD often fail when faced with the need to wait in any given context – and this is precisely where a simple gratification mechanism can have a hugely important role. In fact, it explains how situations featuring long waiting times acquire negative tones through their association with unpleasant emotions elicited by frequent prior experiences of failure. That is why it is so important to gratify children with ADHD, even for small instances of good behaviour. One of the recommendations that parents receive (as discussed in more detail in Chapters 3 and 4) is that they try to keep rebuking their children for misbehaving to a minimum, ignoring any minor episodes, and focus as much as possible on their good behaviours. Appreciating their efforts and gratifying them can improve these children's self-esteem and motivate them to do better.

Conclusions

So, to sum up the content of this chapter, we could say that we still have no unequivocal and thorough explanation for ADHD. The various disciplines and different approaches taken to studying the disorder are like the pieces of a puzzle that we are painstakingly putting together to complete a very complex picture. All these pieces of the puzzle point in the same direction, however, indicating that the behavioural symptoms of ADHD are related to areas of the brain responsible for control, planning and certain complex cognitive tasks (e.g. executive functions). In addition, to being physiologically slightly different from those of typically developing children, these brain areas are rich in receptors for neurotransmitters such as dopamine, which serve specifically to activate them. We now know that the genes governing dopamine receptors and transporters have a part to play, and are probably responsible when dopamine levels in the intersynaptic spaces are inadequate, making it difficult for the neurons in these areas to communicate with one another. Simply put, the brain regions responsible for higher-order tasks, such as inhibitory control and behavioural self-regulation, are less active than normal. This would explain the symptoms typical of ADHD, such as inattention, hyperactivity and impulsivity. We shall see in the following pages that all therapeutic efforts – be they pharmacological or psychological – are designed to activate these brain areas to achieve an adequate level of self-regulation in children with ADHD.

Finally, it is worth mentioning that neuroimaging techniques (such as magnetic resonance) and genetic investigations are used not to obtain a diagnosis of ADHD, but to conduct studies for the purpose of clarifying the neurological foundations of the disorder.

References

Barkley, R. A. (1997). Behavioral inhibition, sustained attention, and executive functions: Constructing a unifying theory of ADHD. *Psychological Bulletin, 121*, 65–94.

Castellanos, F. X., & Tannock, R. (2002). Neuroscience of attention-deficit/hyperactivity disorder: The search for the endophenotype. *Nature Review Neuroscience, 3*, 617–628.

Faraone, S. V., & Larsson, H. (2018). Genetics of attention deficit hyperactivity disorder. *Molecular Psychiatry, 24*, 562–575.

Marzocchi, G. M., Re, A. M., & Cornoldi, C. (2019). Disturbo di Attenzione/Iperattività. In C. Cornoldi (a cura di), *Difficoltà e Disturbi dell'Apprendimento* (pp. 301–331). Bologna, Italy: Il Mulino.

Pennington, B. F., & Ozonoff, S. (1996). Executive functions and developmental psychopathology. *Journal of Child Psychology and Psychiatry, 1*, 51–87.

Sergeant, J., & Van der Meere, J. (1990). Additive factor method applied to psychopathology with special reference to childhood hyperactivity. *Acta Psychologica, 74*, 277–295.

Sergeant, J. A., Van der Meere, J. J., & Oosterlaan, J. (1999). Information processing and energetic factors in attention-deficit/hyperactivity disorder. In H. C. Quay & A. Hogan (Eds.), *Handbook of disruptive behavior disorders* (pp. 75–104). New York: Plenum Press.

Sonuga-Barke, E. J., Bitsakou, P., & Thompson, M. (2010). Beyond the dual pathway model: Evidence for the dissociation of timing, inhibitory, and delay-related impairments in attention-deficit/hyperactivity disorder. *Journal of the American Academy of Child & Adolescent Psychiatry, 49*(4), 345–355.

Willcutt, E. G., Doyle, A. E., Nigg, J. T., Faraone, S. V., & Pennington, B. F. (2005). Validity of the executive function theory of attention-deficit/hyperactivity disorder: A meta-analytic review. *Biological Psychiatry, 57*, 1336–1346.

Chapter 3

Living with ADHD

Introduction

Imagine being an extremely lively seven-year-old and always having dozens of ideas buzzing around in your head. You start doing one thing but then think of something else, so you abandon the first thing you were doing and move on to the next. Imagine feeling as if you had a little "internal motor" always turning at top speed that prevents you from ever sitting still, whatever you are doing. Then imagine the things that seven-year-olds have to do: they go to school, where they are asked to do one task at a time, to keep still, stay seated and concentrate on the various school activities; they have to stand in line and wait to go for lunch, outside for recreation or to the gym. Also bear in mind that seven-year-olds are expected to be reasonably independent: they should be able to get ready for school in the mornings, and know what to put in their schoolbag; they need to bring home all the things they took to school; and so on. Then think of these children playing in the park with their friends, or training at the gym: they are expected to obey the rules of the game, respect other companions' decisions and complete one game before starting another. Can you imagine a child with the features described in the previous chapters being able to fulfil all these expectations? Can children who are always lost in their own thoughts, constantly in motion or exceptionally lively comply with all the demands of the environment and society in which they live? I think not. Children with ADHD suffer because they are unable to satisfy the expectations of the people around them. They usually feel inadequate as a result of being scolded all the time by adults (and sometimes even by their peers). As mentioned in Chapter 1, one of the criteria (according to the DSM-5) for establishing a diagnosis of ADHD is that the symptoms of the condition clearly and evidently interfere with daily life. Moments of inattention, hyperactivity and impulsivity are very common in the general population. Many people can be impulsive, restless or easily distracted. What distinguishes them from individuals with ADHD is that, when necessary, they can control their behaviour. Some people may tend to live their lives "with their head in the clouds", but when they have to complete an important task they succeed in remaining focused and doing it properly. Some people may seem hyperactive because they are constantly engaging in dozens of activities, but they may manage to complete them all efficiently. In other words, such people who are easily distracted or very lively do not have ADHD because these personality traits do not interfere with their performance in their daily lives – unlike what happens with children who have the disorder. It is fair to say that the distinction may sometimes be quite subtle, and it may be diffi-cult for parents or teachers to gauge whether a given child has ADHD or not. That is why there are specialists (such as psych-ologists) who can help differentiate between mere individual differences and genuine behavioural problems. Specialists can use various tools to clarify the picture and advise the family on the most appropriate treatment for any children with symp-toms of ADHD. These youngsters – in addition to having a syndrome – could have a radiant smile, and are witty, affec-tionate and generous. They are children with their own par-ticular features and we should never forget that they are all unique in the way their symptoms combine with their person-alities, so there is no standard protocol applicable to every case of ADHD. It is up to the specialist and the family to assess each situation and judge how best to intervene, bearing in mind the particular characteristics and needs of the child concerned.

What happens at home

For the parents, living with a child who has ADHD can often be very demanding and frustrating. Children with this disorder are difficult to manage, usually even from a very early age. A while ago, one mother made an impression on me when, in describing how difficult she found it to cope with her child, she said:

> This boy gave me problems as soon as he was born. When I was still in hospital after giving birth, the nurses would always bring him to me in my room because he cried so much he woke all the other babies in the nursery!

Another mother told me that, while still in the maternity ward after having her baby, she realized that the newborn a nurse brought her one day could not be her son because he was not crying hard enough. Of course, these are memories reconstructed with the benefit of hindsight and may have been somewhat exaggerated, given the time that had elapsed since the episode occurred. Nonetheless, while these two anecdotes might make us smile, they also give us an idea of the level of stress that the parents of children with ADHD often experience.

There are many aspects that can pose problems for these parents, whose reactions and behaviours can become inappropriate, inconsistent, uncertain, anxious, resigned and so on. The symptoms of inattention, hyperactivity and impulsivity that characterize the disorder can badly disrupt the relationship between parent and child, adding to the parents' stress and frustration. Children with ADHD respond poorly to the "classical" methods for raising children, which implicitly include the expectation that children understand how to behave in certain situations. Generally speaking, when five-year-olds who do not have ADHD see their younger brothers take one of their toys, they give them a shove. Their mothers then scold them, saying something like: "If you push your brother, you'll be in trouble. But if you play nicely with him for ten minutes, I'll get you an ice-cream". By the time these same typically developing children are 14 years old, they may get cross when they see their brothers touching their computers but they think: "If I give him a punch, I might hurt him". They do not want to do that, partly because they love their little brothers and partly because they know their parents would be upset and disappointed with them. In other words, children who do not suffer from ADHD interiorize social rules as they grow up. They gradually learn to exert the same control over their behaviour as their parents or other adults in the room would, developing a good degree of self-regulation in the process.

The situation is different for children with ADHD, who have specific self-regulation difficulties. It takes them longer to interiorize (i.e. to adopt as their own) their parents' behaviour-controlling role, and they need to use special strategies to succeed. That is why parents and other reference figures have a fundamental part to play. If the more "classical" parenting methods are adopted, it becomes difficult to escape a vicious circle of misdeeds on the part of the children and admonishments voiced by the parents. These children have to live not only with their symptoms of ADHD, but also with the frustration of being unable to do what everyone else expects of them at their age. They are never able to please their parents, but they fail to understand why this happens.

To make matters worse, with time their parents may develop misconceptions (e.g. "my son misbehaves deliberately" or "I'm a failure as a parent") that can negatively influence not only how they manage their child's upbringing, but also the family's quality of life as a whole. The causes to which we attribute events can strongly affect how we react to situations, and all the consequences of our actions. If parents become convinced that their children behave badly deliberately to spite them, they will naturally feel hurt and angry. This will probably make them react badly, but scolding and punishments often trigger further negative emotions, more anger and frustration, undermining the self-esteem of parents and children alike, damaging their relationship and creating a very tense and stressful, even exasperated atmosphere for the whole family. On the other hand, parents who attribute their children's troublesome behaviour to their own parenting methods will feel they have failed in their role as parents and tend to "give up", to let matters drop. They let their children have their own way because it seems pointless to do otherwise.

It may also happen that children are punished or rebuked in a manner proportional not to the gravity of what they have done wrong, but to how much their parents are tired and stressed, so the children receive an ambiguous message. For instance, I once spent a day at the beach with a group of friends, including a little boy (3–4 years old) with his father. The boy was being naughty all morning for countless silly reasons, and his father was doing his best to make him behave. At one point, probably because he was tired of hearing the child whining about something or other, the father rebuked him very crossly and the child burst into tears. A minute or two later (probably because he was feeling guilty), the father bought the boy an ice-cream and the child stopped crying as if by magic. This example of daily life goes to show how our behaviour is often driven by the emotion of the moment: when we lose our temper with our children, we punish them regardless of what they have actually done; then we feel guilty so we give them something nice to console them (a sort of reward), regardless of what they have done. This type of behaviour sends children an ambiguous message that they may interpret as: "If I cry hard and long enough, then mummy/daddy will weaken in the end and buy me what I want". This is an example of what Patterson (1982) calls the "coercive cycle", which explains how parents and their children influence one another, especially in stressful situations. Sometimes the parents' reactions unwittingly have the effect of reinforcing their child's bad behaviours, generating a negative spiral that intensifies the problem. For the children involved, the family environment thus becomes the worst place to learn how to deal with difficult situations in their relationships with others (see Box 3.1).

Box 3.1 Recommendations for managing children with ADHD

While I am well aware of how difficult it is to always control ourselves, for children with ADHD it is especially important for there to be consistency in our behaviour, for the most important issues at least. Unfortunately, children with ADHD often test their parents' patience to the limit, so it is entirely normal for their reactions to be governed by their own state of mind rather than by any rules. In actual fact, the keyword for parents must always be "self-control". They must avoid at all cost raising their voices, using vulgar or offensive language, and hitting the child. All their efforts must be channelled into creating a family atmosphere that is calm and peaceful. It is essential to remember that all children tend to adopt the behaviour, attitudes and reactions that they see in their parents, who – for better or worse – are always their role models. The family's educational climate needs to aim for consistency and a strong agreement between the parents, so that they are aligned regarding the behavioural rules they teach their children and want them to obey. If this is not the case, the children's sense of confusion and uncertainty can only increase, and so will their inappropriate behaviour as a consequence. It is generally recommended that parents rebuke their children and punish them as little as possible, but always for the same types of misbehaviour that they judge particularly negative (and subject to agreeing what these are with the child concerned). This enables the children to always receive the same feedback about their behaviour, which helps them to learn self-regulation, and it also makes it easier for the parents to be consistent. To give an example, hitting their little brother warrants punishment (even if the little brother was making a nuisance of himself) because using physical force against somebody is always the wrong way to behave. This gives children a precise idea of which types of behaviour should always be avoided.

The situation is often further aggravated by unhelpful comments and suggestions arriving from elsewhere, from relatives or teachers. Sadly, there is a common conviction that if a child's behaviour is troublesome, it is because their parents have not brought them up properly. The parents consequently feel they are being criticized, even by relatives, friends and teachers, and this not only adds to their sense of frustration but also isolates them socially. To avoid being judged by others, such parents begin to stay away from pleasant social gatherings, such as eating out, attending cultural events for families and so on. All this cannot fail to exacerbate a situation that is already difficult to manage. Parents have told us many a time of feeling anxious when they go to collect their children from school because they expect the teacher to be there, waiting to tell them what problems their child has caused in class during the day. That is why, when these parents meet other parents who have the same problems – at parent training course (which we describe in more detail in Chapter 4), for instance – they often feel enormously relieved. It as if they are finally able to see, for the first time in years, that they are not alone. It is not that they did everything wrong in bringing up their child, and they can stop feeling so guilty if, now and again, they become so tired and frustrated that they wish the child would just go away for a while.

What happens at school

Remaining seated for hours at their desks, listening to lessons without becoming distracted and doing the exercises the teacher assigns them are all extremely difficult tasks for children with ADHD because they have a short sustained-attention span, they are readily distracted and they are constantly fidgeting. These situations consequently give rise to the onset of various types of disruptive behaviour that disturb both the teacher and the other children in the class. For instance, children with ADHD may keep interrupting the teacher to make irrelevant comments, get up without reason, chat with their classmates or be constantly be making noise in the background. I remember one occasion when I was conducting a group activity with some children with ADHD and one of them started singing. I asked the child to stop, because otherwise the others would not be able to hear me explain the activity I was organizing. The child stopped immediately and apologized. Minutes later he started singing again, and when I again asked him to stop he gave me a bewildered look and said: "Why, was I singing again?". Though it may seem hard to believe, this sort of thing happens much more often than we might expect. In other words, children with ADHD quite often behave in certain ways without even being aware of what they are doing; it was not their intention to challenge authority or disturb other people. This is clearly often difficult to accept for a teacher (who also has to manage the needs of a whole class), or for classmates who are trying to concentrate on their school work.

The emotions that teachers may experience in dealing with children who have ADHD can vary. They often feel frustrated because these children seem to have no respect for their role as a teacher, and because they are unable to handle these children. Some teachers even fear the possible consequences of such children's erratic behaviour (Marzocchi & Bongarzone, 2019). So, there are plenty of reasons why these children are scolded by adults or quarrel with other children at school. They are often rebuked by teachers for failing to comply with even the most basic social rules in class (such as staying seated at their desks), and these verbal reprimands then prompt the teacher to write notes for the children to take home to their parents. All this generates high levels of frustration in all parties in the triad: the child feels inadequate, and sometimes even unjustly punished; the teacher feels powerless, and consequently demands some sort of intervention on the part of the parents; and the parents feel defeated, and sometimes disoriented because they simply do not know what to do with the child – especially at school, where they are not even present. Here again, what often happens is an escalation of negative effects: the teacher becomes increasingly severe, rebukes the child more and more often, and writes almost daily notes to the parents. In addition to undermining the children's self-esteem (they begin to feel like the "black sheep" of the class), such behaviour also weakens the effect of any disciplinary action on the children concerned. It is not unusual for children with ADHD to tell me during a session: "You know, I've already had 20 notes and we are only in October!". A teacher's written note should have repercussions at home, but parents often say to me: "He's already being punished for his behaviour at home. He's not allowed to play with his videogames. He can't use his mobile phone, can't watch television … what else can we take away from him?". Clearly, if used repeatedly, this type of action becomes meaningless.

Sometimes children with ADHD also feel like scapegoats because, whenever there is a bit of confusion in class, the teacher always accuses them of being responsible rather than (or more than) other children. If we add to these situations all the times when children with ADHD are disruptive without even being aware of it, we can easily to see why they are always in the teacher's sights.

As we said in Chapter 1, children with ADHD experience all this constant criticism as a succession of small failings, which with time can lead to real problems of self-esteem, especially as they grow older. Here again, when we run teacher-training courses, or simply have meetings with teachers, we explain how important it is to establish a sort of scale of behavioural issues, and we urge them to only scold the children for the most severe or important. We shall see in more detail later on how these strategies can be implemented in class, but the goal must always be to give the children suggestions or, better still, feedback on their behaviour to help them develop self-regulation strategies.

We need to bear in mind that school is also the place where children learn to socialize, deal with their peers and establish their first friendly relationships. We have already mentioned in Chapter 1 that socializing can often be difficult for children with ADHD. We have seen that various aspects of their behaviour can make their company not very pleasant for their peers. They are disruptive in class, constantly moving about (and often disturbing others in the process). They always want to dictate the rules of the game, and so on. Given such characteristics, children with ADHD certainly do not make ideal friends. There are times when other children wrongly accuse them of causing trouble, and point to them as being responsible for misbehaviour even when they were not involved. If a teacher grants them any extra freedom, such as the chance to move around the class during lessons or to go outside to rest for a moment, they are labelled as the "teacher's pet" and their classmates complain about them having certain "privileges". I have thankfully also seen many exemplary situations where teachers succeeded in explaining the difficulties and needs of children with ADHD to the rest of the class, and their companions proved very cooperative and more than willing to help the children concerned. If teachers can create a climate of mutual support and cooperation, children usually know how to respond splendidly and help each other out. The advice of another child in a group is also far more effective than any instructions, punishments or prizes that an adult might give (and we investigate these aspects in more detail in Chapter 6).

Communications between the school and the family

We know that, for any child, their two most important worlds are their family and their school. It goes without saying that these two worlds should interact to offer children the best possible setting in which to grow up. Unfortunately, however, when it comes to children with ADHD, schools and families are often at loggerheads with one another, each accusing the other of failing to manage and educate the child properly. As we have seen, the way children with ADHD behave poses a huge challenge to any adult's psychological balance, so it is quite common for communications between schools and families to flounder. Teachers often seek the parents' cooperation and want to explain their child's troublesome behaviour, but parents experience these exchanges as a criticism of their parenting methods. Vice versa, parents complain that teachers do not know how to manage their child, that their educational strategies are too strict and have little effect, and that they fail to follow the family's advice.

That said, when parents and teachers do succeed in cooperating effectively, they can achieve good results. There is generally a clinician who acts as a mediator, especially to help the two parties set shared goals and to coordinate the educational strategies to use in the two different settings. A very simple but useful example is what goes rather charmingly by the name of a "logbook": this is an exercise book used for communications between the children's families and their teachers. Instead of using teacher's notes in the child's school diary (which can look like a "written rebuke"), the purpose of the logbook is to give an account of the child's behaviour – in class or at home – especially as regards goals shared by the parents and teachers. For instance, let us imagine that one such goal is to get the child to take all the materials they need for their lessons to school without help. Parents can make a note in the logbook to let the teacher know if their child prepared their schoolbag unassisted, and if they made a fuss about having to do so. Next day, teachers can add a comment to let the parents know whether their child succeeded in bringing everything they needed for their lessons, or if something was missing.

What happens in adolescence

Teenagers with ADHD tend to reveal mainly attentional difficulties and impulsiveness, while any hyperactivity they showed as children is converted into an internal agitation, a sense of restlessness, that gives these individuals a particularly strong desire for freedom. They always want to decide for themselves what to do. As they go through the experience of puberty they can suffer from an intense emotional instability. They often struggle to understand themselves and the world around them.

At this age, their impulsivity may become apparent in various ways. They may not study for class tests until the last minute, even only the night before. When their mothers ask them to take out the rubbish or come and have breakfast, they may say: "Sure, I'll be right there!", but minutes later they have completely forgotten what they were asked to do, and may be found busy watching television, playing video games or on their phones.

Their attentional difficulties are particularly obvious when these teenagers go to their rooms, often with every intention of studying and doing their homework, but instead they start daydreaming, toying with things on their desk, gazing out of the window and doing everything except their school work. Another typical situation is when they start doing a test or some boring activity in class and their attention is drawn to something else, so they leave the initial task incomplete, or have to rush to finish, achieving poor results. More in general, adolescents with ADHD may embark on a number of hobbies or creative activities, only to abandon them all after a little while.

Because of their particular characteristics, these young people soon tire of scarcely stimulating, repetitive activities, especially homework, boring jobs and hobbies that demand lots of practice, and they even lose interest in their friends. They often go in search of novel experiences and excitement, something to keep their interest alive. This can lead them towards innocent activities such as rollerblading, dancing, playing with the PlayStation or racing on their bicycles, but it can also lend appeal to more risk-taking behaviour, such as experimenting with alcohol and drugs, sexual promiscuity, shoplifting or violence.

Poor planning, forgetfulness and a difficulty with the retrieval of previously learned information are problems that make adolescents with ADHD arrive unprepared to class, or without the school materials they need. They do their homework hurriedly at the last minute, or fail to do it at all. They make mistakes when noting in their diaries what work they should do. They leave their bedrooms very untidy and fail to keep track of any long-term commitments. In addition to organizational and planning problems, they have a distorted perception of time. While working on a task, they do not realize how much time has elapsed or how much time they have left to complete it. This can make them unable to programme their days. When we think that adolescents usually engage in various out-of-school activities, and are expected to manage their commitments without help, it is easy to guess what happens to those with ADHD. They are often late and they forget what they had promised to do, so they give the impression of being unreliable, and this makes them give up many of their chosen pastimes.

From an emotional standpoint, adolescents with ADHD usually react to stressful situations by going in one of two directions, either they become aggressive or they become depressed. Another typical trait is their tendency to give spontaneous expression to any ill humour, whatever the situation they are in. They are unable to assess situations calmly, or carefully analyse their thoughts. Instead they react without thinking, often with an oppositional response or contrary argument (see Box 3.2 for the evolution of comorbidities).

Box 3.2 The evolution of comorbidities

In childhood, ADHD can be associated with a number of academic, behavioural, family, emotional, social and developmental difficulties that are encountered to a greater degree in children with this syndrome, but are not among its diagnostic symptoms. These problems often increase exponentially with the onset of adolescence, when expectations concerning these young people's performance are greater. In some cases, the problems become severe enough to be considered as comorbidities and thus contribute to a psychiatric syndrome; in others they may still be significant problems, but they do not converge into a diagnostic category.

From what we have said so far, it is also easy to imagine that another context in which adolescents with ADHD have numerous problems concerns their academic performance. If they have no comorbid learning disabilities, children with ADHD succeed in getting by at primary school, albeit with a few issues. But then they are very likely to encounter greater difficulties when they move on to secondary school. This is when not only the students' academic burden increases, but also their need to work autonomously and to plan their activities. Adolescents with ADHD continue instead to manage their commitments in their usual way. They are hasty in doing their school work, ignoring important details and making mistakes because they become distracted. Students have more teachers and more subjects to study, so they need to be better organized and know how to manage their homework and various school subjects without help.

The greatest difficulty for adolescents with ADHD consists in completing their school work and handing it in on time. This may be due not only to a cognitive overloading of their organizational and executive abilities, but also because they frequently have specific learning disorders, in reading and mathematics, written expression and other areas. Some learning difficulties have a stronger influence in secondary school than in primary school because secondary-school students are expected to express their ideas and thoughts in written form (something not required of pupils in primary school). Adolescents with ADHD who also have problems with written expression may come up against their first difficulties in secondary school when they need to write essays, or at the time of their final exams. In other cases, their learning difficulties may emerge earlier on, for example if their impairment affects their memory, planning or simply the ability to pay attention in class. Students with ADHD and an above-average IQ can often effortlessly complete their primary-school education, but they cannot hope to do equally well at secondary school or university, which both demand many hours of study and the utmost concentration. This typical situation goes to show why ADHD is often only diagnosed after an individual has reached adolescence or even in early adulthood. An example of this situation comes from Mark's story.

Mark is 12 years old. His brother has been diagnosed with ADHD of the predominantly attention-deficit subtype. When Mark starts his first year of secondary school, his parents notice that his academic performance has deteriorated and so (also at a teacher's suggestion) they decide to have him assessed. When Mark comes to me, he tells me about the terrible struggle he has with his studies, his relationship with his many teachers (who all have different demands and use different methods) and his class-mates. He explains how different it is from primary school, where he only had two teachers, who were very helpful and attentive. These primary-school teachers made the children work together, helping to improve the relationship between them. They made sure that almost all the activities were completed in class and there was very little homework to do. In primary school, Mark served as class secretary, and this enabled him to be better organized and always know what homework was required.

Now things have changed completely: he has numerous teachers who often give them lots of homework, which they assign in the last two minutes of the lesson when the bell is ring-ing and everybody is talking, so Mark never knows exactly what he is supposed to do at home. There are lots of pages to study, even about things not explained in class. Mark easily becomes distracted while reading, finding after half an hour that he can only remember what he read on the first four or five lines. There are lots of essays to write and, although he has plenty of ideas spinning around in his head, once put to paper they are not very clear, the content is disorganized and there are lots of mistakes in the tenses of his verbs. This whole situation, combined with his relational difficulties with his teachers and new classmates, makes Mark feel low and demotivated.

Combined with their academic difficulties, behavioural problems are the main issue associated with ADHD in adolescence. Given that a tendency for rebellion is normal for everyone going through this delicate stage of development, it is hard for parents to distinguish between what is "natural" adolescent behaviour and what is a trait associated with ADHD. The behaviour of a small proportion of adolescents with ADHD poses more serious problems: they may tell lies, steal, skip school and become physically aggressive. These youngsters are often diagnosed with conduct disorder.

The academic and behavioural problems that teenagers with ADHD experience inevitably lead to clashes within the family. The parents of typically developing adolescents have to cope with moments of greater conflict in the early years of puberty too, but this delicate developmental stage is generally much more intense for the parents of children with ADHD. Their confrontations are characterized by communication difficulties (mutual accusations, going on the defensive, abrupt interruptions, avoiding eye contact, refusing to listen, lecturing and the like) and inappropriate conflict-solving behaviour (arbitrary stances, failure to negotiate). Parents may sometimes give up trying to control their teenage children, who in turn may exploit this situation by ceasing to try and evading their responsibilities, thus achieving their objectives.

ADHD and sleep

Another characteristic of young people with ADHD that can make family life difficult is the trouble they have in regulating their sleeping patterns. Sleep disorders associated with ADHD pose an important problem for both the young people and their families because they can negatively affect these adolescents' academic performance and aggravate their symptoms of ADHD.

A meta-analysis found that in 25–55% of cases, the parents of adolescents with ADHD describe them as having trouble falling asleep, frequently waking during the night and being over-active in the evenings and at night (De Crescenzo et al., 2016). In particular, their difficulty with falling asleep could stem from an altered circadian rhythm due to a delay in the peak secretion of melatonin (a substance produced by a gland at the base of the brain that governs our sleeping–waking cycles).

The sleeping difficulties of adolescents with ADHD can be quite persistent. A recently published study considered the sleep problems associated with ADHD over a period of 12 months: the results showed that they are generally transient, but they persist in one in every ten cases. A risk factor for persistent sleep disorders would be the joint presence (comorbidity) of behavioural disorders with symptoms of depression and anxiety (Gregory, Agnew-Blais, Matthews, Moffitt, & Arseneault, 2017).

It is important to recognize and treat sleep disorders associated with ADHD. A professional should conduct an accurate, long-term clinical assessment of the issues reported by the parents because there may be other causes going undiagnosed (such as obstructive sleep apnea syndrome). But the first step towards treating sleep disorders is to establish good "sleep hygiene" practices. This involves adopting a ritual for falling asleep: going to bed at the same time; reducing the intensity of the lighting and noise in the home; avoiding drinks containing caffeine, theophylline or alcohol; and avoiding napping too frequently or for too long during the day, especially towards evening (see Box 3.3).

Box 3.3 Suggestions for a good sleep hygiene

Below is a more detailed list of useful suggestions for good sleep hygiene, especially in adolescence (Sanavio, 2006).

1. GO TO BED ONLY WHEN YOU FEEL REALLY SLEEPY and are struggling to keep your eyes open. Do not go to bed in the hope that you will fall asleep sooner or later. If you are not feeling really tired, spend some time doing something else, preferably useful or pleasant, but not stimulating (e.g. a warm bath, easy reading, relaxing music). The idea is that it is better to go to bed at 3.00 and fall asleep within five or ten minutes, than to go to bed at midnight and then not fall asleep until 3.00.

2. ONLY USE YOUR BED FOR SLEEPING. Do not use it for other activities, such as studying, using your mobile phone, reading and so on. It is important to find somewhere else for these activities, preferably in another room.

3. DO NOT LIE AWAKE IN BED FOR MORE THAN 20 MINUTES. If you cannot fall asleep, then it is best to get up after 20 minutes and, if possible, go to another room to do something else. It is important to wait for a signal from your body (heavy eyelids and muscles) before going back to bed. This helps your mind to associate bed with sleeping and recognize the signs of imminent sleep onset, distinguishing them from other feelings of tiredness and fatigue. Continue to follow this rule even several times over: one sleepless night is no real issue.

4. If you wake during the night, DO NOT WAIT TOO LONG TO GET BACK TO SLEEP. It is better to get up and go somewhere else or to another room. It can be useful to find a place where you can spend some time awake in the middle of the night, listening to music or engaging in some pleasant pastime.

5. ALWAYS GET UP AT THE SAME TIME. Keep your waking time constant even if the time you go to sleep varies. This helps you to readjust your internal clock, which controls your sleeping–waking cycle, and to gradually synchronize the time you fall asleep. Bear in mind that developing good sleeping habits takes time, patience and consistency.

6. AVOID NAPPING DURING THE DAY.

7. AVOID DEMANDING OR STIMULATING PHYSICAL OR MENTAL ACTIVITIES BEFORE BEDTIME. Identify which activities you find stimulating (studying certain subjects, reading certain books) and which ones you find relaxing or boring (other types of book, a warm bath, music, muscle relaxation techniques), and use the latter in an unwinding phase to prepare for sleep.

8. AVOID DISTURBING THOUGHTS. If you have thoughts that could interfere with your sleep, you need to find a place and a time for thinking about them so that this place is not in bed, and the right time is not at bedtime. It is a good idea to try and set the right emotional tone, and give the right weight to any worries that prevent you from sleeping.

References

De Crescenzo, F., Licchelli, S., Ciabattini, M., Menghini, D., Armando, M., Alfieri, P., & Quested, D. (2016). The use of actigraphy in the monitoring of sleep and activity in ADHD: A meta-analysis. *Sleep Medicine Reviews*, 26, 9–20.

Gregory, A. M., Agnew-Blais, J. C., Matthews, T., Moffitt, T. E., & Arseneault, L. (2017). ADHD and sleep quality: Longitudinal analyses from childhood to early adulthood in a twin cohort. *Journal of Clinical Child and Adolescent Psychology: the official journal of the Society of Clinical Child and Adolescent Psychology, American Psychological Association, Division 53*, 46(2), 284–294.

Marzocchi, G. M., & Bongarzone, E. (2019). *Disattenti e iperattivi: Cosa possono fare genitori e insegnanti*. Bologna: Il Mulino.

Patterson, G. R. (1982). *Coercive family process*. Eugene, OR: Castalia.

Sanavio, E. (2006). *Come vincere l'insonnia*. Firenze, Italy: Giunti Editore.

Chapter 4

The most-often-used treatments

A multifocal approach

Introduction

Intervention for ADHD is just as complex and delicate as the disorder itself. As we have seen in previous chapters, ADHD is a pervasive disorder. In other words, it affects every aspect and every context of a child's life. That is why there is unanimous agreement that it is fundamentally important to take a multifocal approach to its treatment, involving not only the children affected, but also their families and their schools, i.e. the life contexts in which children and adolescents spend most of their time. It is important for the goals adopted and the action taken in one setting (the family) to be consistent with those in the other (at school). All interventions should then be discussed with the psychologist and with the child concerned. It is usually the psychologist who chooses, coordinates and mediates the type of intervention, which can be quite complex.

Treatment for ADHD can involve various professional figures because two types of intervention are feasible for this disorder – one pharmacological, the other psychological (or psycho-educational) – and they are often used together.

In the 1980s, it was mainly in the United States that clinicians were treating ADHD with medication, while doctors in Europe were much less inclined to do so. Psychotherapeutic interventions were preferred, especially in Italy. Among the efforts to clarify which type of intervention is more effective, one of the most important studies was conducted in the United States. This was the Multimodal Treatment Study of Children with ADHD (MTA) coordinated by the National Institute of Mental Health. It involved 579 children with ADHD from seven to nine years old, together with their families and schools, and it was designed to compare the various treatment options. The interventions considered were:

- psychological and behavioural treatments (parent training, behavioural psycho-educational treatment for the children, and training and supervision for the teachers);
- pharmacological treatment;
- combined pharmacological and psychological treatment.

To judge the efficacy of these three types of approach, there was also a control group that simply followed the paediatrician's advice. The four groups involved in the study were closely monitored for 14 months, with follow-up assessments to ascertain the maintenance of any results. The study findings were reported in various scientific articles, the first of which was published in 1999 (MTA group, 1999a). They showed that pharmacological therapy and the combined treatment were more effective than psychological and behavioural treatments alone, and that children in the combined treatment group benefited more than those only treated pharmacologically, particularly as regards improvements in their social relations (Hinshaw et al., 2000; MTA Cooperative Group, 1999b; Wells et al., 2000). It is worth noting that the children in the combined treatment group were given an approximately 20% lower dose of medication (Swanson et al., 2002), and the degree of satisfaction expressed by their parents and teachers was significantly higher than in the other groups that were given psychological or pharmacological treatment alone (Arnold et al., 2004). Finally, the improvements observed in the first 14 months tended to fade with time in all three groups. Even improvements obtained with a strict and intensive pharmacological treatment were not maintained in the months after completing the therapeutic protocol.

An important take-home message emerging from an analysis of the results of the MTA study and other research in this field is that any treatment must involve families and schools, as well as the children with ADHD, to ensure that all the people who contribute to these children's education are well-informed, active and cooperative. The cognitive-behavioural approach seems to be the most effective type of psychological treatment, especially if it is part of a multifocal intervention that includes the child, the parents and the teachers. Another conclusion that we can draw from the American study is that, although pharmacological treatment can produce some immediate (and sometimes remarkable) results, it is not enough to deal with such a complex and lasting problem as ADHD.

Another issue to consider is that the improvements faded over time after the intervention came to an end. This finding makes us realize that any intervention to treat ADHD needs to be repeated at various times, accompanying the children affected as they grow up. As we saw in previous chapters, the disorder is chronic and it changes as the child develops, so it is often a good idea to take up the therapeutic care pathway again at various important stages of their life. We have already mentioned several times that some of these stages coincide with the passage from one type of school to the next, because the demands of the environment often increase and children with ADHD need help to adjust to their new reality.

In the following pages we briefly review the types of intervention used for children with ADHD and the main life settings in which they are used.

Pharmacological therapy

This is not the ideal place for a thorough analysis of the pharmacological therapies available for ADHD, but a few brief comments are warranted. There are essentially two macrocategories of drugs for this condition, some of which are psychoactive and others are not. Psychoactive drugs are currently considered the most effective for the treatment of ADHD. The active ingredient in most psychoactive drugs used in this setting is methylphenidate (which is also the drug that has been tested the most). Among the non-psychoactive drugs, the most often used is atomoxetine.

Methylphenidate takes effect on the modulation of dopamine reuptake. In Chapter 2, we explained the neurophysiological factors involved in ADHD: dopamine is a neurotransmitter active in areas of the brain (especially the prefrontal cortex) that regulate certain higher cognitive functions, such as our capacity for control, planning, attention and so on. Methylphenidate regulates the quantity of this neurotransmitter needed in these areas of the brain. Various studies have shown that methylphenidate is effective both in improving the performance of children with ADHD in specific cognitive tasks (such as planning, sustained attention, etc.) and in containing their behavioural symptoms (improving their attention span and reducing their inattentive and hyperactive behaviour). This drug has proved useful in around 70% of patients with ADHD, although there is a considerable variability in different individuals' response.

Just like any other drug, methylphenidate can also have some side effects, such as loss of appetite, insomnia, restlessness and stomach ache, although in most cases these side effects improve if the drug dosage is adjusted. The most important side effect, however, is a reduction in growth rate. To limit this effect as far as possible, it is advisable to administer the drug during the school year (when the children benefit the most, as they are more attentive and less hyperactive), and suspend the treatment during the summer to allow them to recover from their growth delay. Coghill and colleagues (2014) conducted a meta-analysis to assess the effect size (ES), i.e. the strength of the relationship between two variables, of the differences in children with ADHD before and after treatment with methylphenidate in their performance of certain tasks in which they usually fared worse than controls. The authors found that methylphenidate treatment had a moderate effect on their working memory (ES = 0.26), slightly improved their mean response times (ES = 0.24), reduced their impulsivity (ES = 0.41) and considerably influenced the variability of their performance in a given task (ES = 0.62). In other words, the children's performance was less erratic, an indication of a more constant level of concentration and focus on the task in hand.

Although psychoactive drugs are the treatment of choice, some children and adolescents with ADHD (roughly 30%) respond to them poorly or not at all, or suffer from severe side effects. That is when other, non-psychoactive drugs such as atomoxetine are used instead. Atomoxetine takes effect on noradrenaline, which regulates attention, impulsivity and activity levels by blocking the reabsorption of norepinephrine. Various studies have confirmed its efficacy (e.g. Tanaka, Rohde, Feldman, & Upadhyaya, 2013). Atomoxetine is administered to children over six, adolescents and adults, usually starting with a low dosage and then raising it, and measuring its overall effects after about 12 weeks. In addition to specific improvements in the symptoms of ADHD, there has been evidence of a partial improvement in social functioning in adolescents. The drug is generally well tolerated, but it does have some side effects, including headache, stomach ache, loss of appetite, nausea and vomiting, and drowsiness. Atomoxetine is also associated with an increase in heart rate and blood pressure, but poses fewer sleeping and growth problems in children than psychoactive drugs. It has also been associated with a lower tendency for abuse than psychoactive drugs, so it may be the treatment of choice for patients at risk of substance abuse issues.

Psychological intervention

The main goal of psychological intervention for ADHD is to improve the individual's overall functioning. This demands action not only on the baseline characteristics of ADHD (attention deficit, hyperactivity and impulsivity), but also on emotional-relational aspects, learning skills and relationships in the family and at school.

Every treatment must be suited to a particular child, and clinicians should take various factors into account in their choice of a given type of intervention, including: any comorbidity with other disorders; the family situation; how well the school cooperates; and so on. It is also important to devise an intervention plan with certain priorities in mind. For instance, a child with ADHD may begin to show signs of severe performance anxiety and loss of self-esteem after a very stressful period involving numerous experiences of failure at school and elsewhere (in sports, for instance). When it comes to this, the priority of any invention is to focus not on the main symptoms of ADHD, but on the problems of anxiety and low self-esteem, which make the clinical picture more complicated and expose the child to the risk of developing full-blown, associated mental disorders.

Intervention with the child

There are various possible types of intervention undertaken with the children themselves. In a meta-analysis, Sonuga-Barke and colleagues (2013) identified several forms of nonpharmacological treatment for ADHD: behavioural therapies (including therapy with the parents, child and teachers); cognitive therapies, mainly focusing on training attention and working memory, which can include both paper-and-pencil and computer-based tasks; neurofeedback; and particular diets (we dedicate a section to this topic at the end of this chapter).

Cognitive-behavioural therapies aim to make children with ADHD more aware of their difficulties, and teach them strategies to improve on their weaknesses. The intervention concentrates on enabling them to acquire a greater awareness of their problems, and to "train" their self-regulation. It should also make children increasingly independent in their search for the best strategies to adopt to deal with their problems in various contexts, to develop their social skills and to reinforce certain cognitive and neuropsychological abilities. A classic, widely-used cognitive-behavioural approach focuses on teaching the child to exert a greater self-control through self-instruction and problem-solving. The assumption is that these techniques are initially implemented deliberately and consciously, then interiorized over time, compensating for a child's inadequate self-regulation. Cognitive treatments aim to enhance the deficient cognitive functions in children with ADHD, which may concern attention, memory, capacity for control and so on. The core idea behind this type of intervention is that, by improving a cognitive dysfunction that lies at the bottom of ADHD, we can positively influence its primary symptoms (inattention, hyperactivity, impulsivity) and sometimes also secondary aspects such as social and academic skills.

Neurofeedback is a technique that uses electrodes positioned on the head to record the electrical activity of an individual's brain in the form of the frequency and amplitude of the brain-waves relating to a given activity that is conducted at the time. These data are transmitted to a computer to convert them into a format that can be displayed on screen and thus encoded by the user. For children, a playful setting is usually adopted, borrowing from the format of video games (e.g. a basketball player who must try to throw the ball into the basket). By means of the feedback shown on the screen, individuals can get to know how their own brain "behaves", and then try to deliberately modify their brain's electrical activity by adopting a certain cognitive state. In this way, they can see what happens and learn to "manage" the feedback relating to a given cognitive activity in order to achieve a certain desired state (e.g. to make the player score a point).

One of the main issues with such treatments for children with ADHD concerns their generalization. In other words, when children are in a highly structured, hetero-regulated setting, where there is an adult who helps them to control their behaviour, as in a psychologist's office, they succeed in working well, keeping their attention focused and controlling their behaviour, and thus obtain good results. The problem is how to obtain the same results in a more natural setting, at home or at school, where the environment is often by no means structured, there are countless sources of distraction, and other people's behaviour can be irritating. Then the children suddenly seem to forget what they learned during their session with the psychologist.

In two recent meta-analyses on these issues (a meta-analysis pools the results of several studies conducted independently on the same topic), the findings of various studies were examined to see whether, and to what degree, cognitive and cognitive-behavioural training could be effective. The first meta-analysis considered the outcomes of intervention focusing on specific cognitive functions that are impaired in children with ADHD, which involved training working memory, inhibition and attention. It showed that these training methods have only modest effects, especially when we consider the most obvious symptoms of ADHD. Simply put, training working memory has positive effects on working memory tasks, but less evident effects on the symptoms of inattention and hyperactivity that children with ADHD experience at home and at school (Cortese et al., 2015). The other meta-analysis considered cognitive-behavioural types of treatment, finding positive effects on the primary symptoms of ADHD (inattention, hyperactivity and impulsivity), parenting quality, school results and social skills. These effects were much more limited, however, when the results obtained were assessed blindly (i.e. by third parties instead of the people directly involved in the treatment). For instance, when parents attend parent training programmes, they answer questionnaires on various aspects of their parenting, how their children's symptoms of ADHD emerge at home and so on. Their child's teachers answer parallel questionnaires specifically to check for any improvements in the child's behaviour in the classroom setting. In this case, the teachers act as blind assessors. To return to the second meta-analysis, the authors reported that the results are more modest when blind assessments are considered.

These findings would again seem to show that it is very difficult for children with ADHD to generalize any improvements from one setting to another. Very often, improvements that parents who have attended a parent training programme see at home are the outcome of changes not only in their children's behaviour, but also in their own (in the way they approach their child, for instance). It is unlikely that such positive changes achieved jointly by the parents and children at home will be spontaneously reflected at school as well. That is why it is essential for the school to be actively involved too, and for the teachers' behaviour to be consistent with what the parents do at home. This helps children with ADHD to implement more appropriate behavioural patterns, and do their very best.

From these studies, it is easy to see the importance of working with the surrounding context. In the ideal treatment, changes that the children achieve with the psychologist during a session should then be reflected at home and also at school.

Intervention with the parents

To succeed in helping children with ADHD, parents have to do something very difficult, and that is change their usual way of thinking. In fact, the first step consists in abandoning our classical reasoning, which implicitly contains the expectation that children know how to behave in certain situations, and adopting an "ADHD way" of reasoning instead, which is better suited to managing children and adolescents diagnosed with this disorder.

This different approach demands a change of perspective for parents, because they need to realize that their child's behaviour – which is often irritating in the majority of cases (they constantly move about when they are asked to sit still, they fail to answer when they are called, they lack self-regulation and act impulsively) – is their normal way of being. To help parents adapt, "parent training" courses are organized not only for the purpose of supporting parents in the difficult task of understanding and educating these very special children, but also to teach them educational techniques that differ from the traditional approach to a child's upbringing. Parent training programmes should break the vicious cycle that we mentioned earlier by teaching parents new ways to interact with their child.

Parent training schemes began more than 40 years ago as a type of intervention to deal with children with behavioural disorders. Taking this approach, the parents are the principal agents of their children's development, and it is essential to use various methods to improve their interaction with their child to facilitate the latter's positive behaviour. In the 1960s, the classic therapy with children was associated with intervention with their parents, especially to deal with cases of phobias, antisocial behaviour and other severe childhood disorders. Right from these early experiences, it became clear that intervention with parents enabled any progress made in therapy with the child to be generalized and remain stable over time. It was also found that parents are capable of modifying any relational styles and attitudes that negatively influence their child's and their family's well-being (Paiano, Re, Ferruzza, & Cornoldi, 2014).

A classic parent training intervention is based on the use of shared life situations and on observation of the child in their natural environment. Applied in this field, the observational method has enabled us to identify environmental causes that can contribute to the troublesome behaviour of children with ADHD. Special importance is attributed to a functional analysis of their behaviour with a view to pinpointing particular factors that tend to act as triggers of problematic behaviour (antecedents) and underscoring the consequences that – though it may not seem so – can be experienced as positive (reinforcing) by the child, and thus contribute to supporting a given troublesome behaviour. This type of behavioural analysis can help us to understand and change certain problematic interactions. When it comes to childhood disorders, parents are often unaware of which factors unleash or contain the onset of an undesirable type of behaviour in their child. Behavioural techniques can be applied to numerous situations in normal daily life, providing there is an awareness of the goals and the limitations of these methods.

Inspired mainly by behavioural psychologists (e.g. Bijou, 1997), this approach makes parents more aware of, and more involved in their child's developmental pathway, partly by means of objective assessments of the child's behaviour in the family setting. Parent training also has the purpose of adding value to the parents' commitment to their role, and supporting their sense of self-efficacy. In this type of approach, parents regain their perception of being the primary agent of change in their child, albeit with a consultant's help. Educational self-efficacy depends on the parents' ability to have an effective role, and on their self-perception in this role. The parenting experience is all the more positive the more parents feel capable of taking care of their children. In this way, they become more satisfied with their efforts, and their self-efficacy increases.

Another important advantage of observing family dynamics is that we sometimes succeed in changing the approach to managing difficult situations through examining them in terms of their causal attributions, i.e. what we perceive as the causes that trigger and explain an event. These causal attributions strongly influence a parent's behaviour. When a child has a tantrum, for instance, their parents' reaction may differ considerably, depending on the explanation (or causal attribution) the parents envisage for their child's behaviour. If they attribute it to a physical illness, they will be more tolerant and may try and keep the child happy. But if they think the tantrum is due to a passing whim, they will certainly be more severe and less likely to satisfy the child's demands. When parents are very tired, they may not pause to wonder why their child is misbehaving, they just want them to stop, so they might let the child have their way without thinking of the consequences. Different causal attributions give rise to different types of behaviour because they are strictly linked to our idea of whether or not we are able to influence a situation. Parents who feel well prepared to deal with problematic situations will take a more positive approach to them. But when they fail, they risk attributing to themselves all the responsibility, without considering any other factors that may have influenced what happened.

Going now into the more technical aspects of parent training for families with children who have ADHD, this consists in a series of meetings organized by a psychologist, who interacts with groups of parents. The goals are usually (Vio, Marzocchi, & Offredi, 1999):

- to SUPPORT parents in their efforts to bring up a child with ADHD;
- to IDENTIFY some common problematic interactions;
- to SUGGEST better strategies for coping with difficult situations;
- to IMPROVE and/or solve problematic situations encountered day-to-day.

From an approach that initially aimed simply to offer parents advice on educational matters, we have gradually moved on to behavioural parent training that is designed to facilitate a better assimilation of the most appropriate educational methods and lead to a genuine change in the parents' behaviour. The techniques most often used for this purpose in behavioural parent training are listed below (and explained in more detail later on):

- modelling (learning through observation);
- role playing (reproducing situations of daily life);

- timeout (suspending reinforcement);
- token economy;
- reinforcement and the cost of the reaction.

As concerns the psycho-educational techniques that have proved effective, Cunningham and colleagues (1995), and Webster-Stratton and colleagues (1996) suggest that using videos and role playing during meetings enables the topics being discussed to be fully understood.

Eyberg and colleagues (1998) concentrated on how difficult it may be for parents to maintain over time the results achieved by the end of a parent training programme. These authors recommend routine "top-up" meetings for the purpose of the parents' self-monitoring, and to provide adequate support for their parenting efforts even after the training has ended.

Fabiano and colleagues (2009) focused on the role of fathers of children with ADHD. They found that involving fathers in their child's activities reduced the child's problematic behavioural traits. In particular, the factors that these authors judged to be most effective were positive reinforcement, timeout and a structured environment.

Jones and colleagues (2007, 2008) developed a project called "Incredible Years, Basic" that involved 133 families with children of preschool age showing traits consistent with ADHD. This programme promoted positive parenting through the use of reinforcement, a greater involvement of parents in their children's pastimes and clearly structured activities. Their results showed an improvement in the children's behaviour, with fewer conduct-related problems and a better-quality parent–child relationship.

Behavioural techniques

Here we briefly explain the principal behavioural techniques used with children who have ADHD. These techniques can be used by parents and teachers alike, providing they have been trained to use them appropriately. It is important to provide a brief explanation of the technical terms used in this context to make the proposed strategies as clear as possible.

Reinforcement. This means some form of gratification awarded immediately for a child's appropriate behaviour. Reinforcement can be practical and tangible, symbolic or socio-affective. It is advisable to use tangible reinforcement for smaller children, such as small gifts, trading cards, stickers and so on. Symbolic and socio-affective reinforcements are more appropriate for older children. Symbolic reinforcements may include smileys or stars, for instance, while socio-affective reinforcements may be compliments or hugs. The choice of the most appropriate reinforcement for a given child also depends on their own personal characteristics. For a reinforcement to be effective it must be:

- immediate;
- related to a specific behaviour;
- given when deserved;
- desirable for the child receiving it;
- variable, to retain its appeal;
- proportional to the behaviour being rewarded.

Cost of the reaction. This consists in denying a child something pleasant when their behaviour is inappropriate. This technique is closely connected to the concept of reinforcement: when children behave appropriately (preferably in a manner explained by the parents and agreed beforehand, such as a rule to obey), they receive a reinforcement; when they misbehave badly (here again, based on a prior agreement with the parents), their reaction carries a "cost" that could involve them having to lose something previously gained as reinforcement (they may have to give back two trading cards, for instance).

These two techniques have the merit of giving the children positive and negative feedback on their behaviour, while enabling parents to avoid having to keep rebuking their children (something to which the children often turn a deaf ear). It is very important, however, to give more positive than negative feedback as this helps the child to understand how best to behave and what is expected of them. It is particularly useful:

- to describe the child's positive behaviour;
- to express appreciation for it.

When children do something right, it is important to tell them so and to be specific. Just to say "Well done!" all the time tends not to promote their positive behaviour. It is more useful to keep our praise for when they really deserve it. Also, saying "You've done a great job" is not the same as saying "Wow! I really like what you've done. You've made me truly happy!". Children generally want to please, and they will be more inclined to repeat a given type of behaviour in future if it has a positive effect on the adults around them.

Token economy. This technique combines reinforcements and costs of reactions to help children learn to regulate their behaviour. It usually involves a written contract between the parents and their child (or between a teacher and a child, or even between a therapist and a child) containing clear rules about how to "earn" reinforcements or pay the "costs" of inappropriate reactions. The token economy must always be associated with more general goals, however. Its specific purpose is to help the child understand what types of behaviour will enable them to reach a certain goal (to succeed in getting ready for bed by themselves, for instance). This technique enables us to avoid constantly rebuking a child, which usually has a negative effect on their self-esteem – and that is why it is also important for the behaviours for which they are rewarded with a "token" to be more numerous than those that make them lose one.

Let us look at a very simple example of a token economy. If the goal is for the child to learn to get ready for bed promptly without help, the contract can be written along the following lines.

Behaviours that are rewarded (reinforcement):

- one mark for going to get ready as soon as mummy or daddy tell you it's time to go to bed;
- one mark for having cleaned your teeth within five minutes;
- one mark for having been to the toilet;
- one mark for having put on your pyjamas;
- one mark for tidying up your clothes;
- one mark for getting into bed.

If children fail to complete one of these desirable behaviours, they simply do not earn a mark. There is no need to punish or rebuke them. Instead, parents can agree with the child that some negative behaviours carry a cost (the cost of the reaction):

- if you don't start to go and get ready for bed after being told three times (you lose one mark);
- if you don't wash your teeth (you lose one mark);
- if you don't want to go to bed (you lose one mark).

Timeout. This is a technique that must only be used in extreme cases and consists in putting a stop to a child's very serious misbehaving. The goal is to prevent an escalation that leads to everyone becoming exasperated. It is a good idea to identify a quiet corner at home or at school where the child can go to calm down and get over the anger they often feel at such moments. It is best for this "timeout" to last a few minutes and, especially if the child is small, for the adult to be there as a calm and reassuring reference figure (the adult should not continue to rebuke the child once they are "on the thinking step"). So, if a parent has also become very angry in these circumstances, they too should take a "timeout", away from the situation and the child, for a minute or two, leaving the other parent with the child.

Modelling. This is a technique that enables children to learn through imitation. It is the method that especially small children use to learn. That is why it is so important for parents to behave as positive models for their children. This concept is explained during parent training programmes, and parents are urged to try as hard as possible to ensure that they behave positively when faced with difficult situations. It is by observing them that their children understand how to behave – how not to be impulsive, for instance.

Role playing. This technique consists in acting out certain situations that are usually troublesome. Some individuals will be the "actors", and others the "audience". This method is used to act out experiences, and the dynamics that can develop in difficult situations can then be analysed by the group. Actors and audience report their experiences and emotions relating to the scene they have depicted or witnessed.

Intervention at school

As we have said several times in this chapter, involving the teachers in the therapeutic process is essential to the success of any treatment for children with ADHD. Systematic meetings between clinicians and teachers must have several goals: to inform teachers about the characteristics of the disorder; to optimize teachers' relationships with their pupils; and to suggest educational strategies to improve the environment for these children at school. It would be best if the whole team of teachers could attend these meetings so that they can adopt a consistent educational approach.

During the meetings, experts have an opportunity to suggest teaching strategies that not only make it easier for children with ADHD to learn, but also and most importantly improve these children's relationships with their classmates and teachers. It is through the teachers' intervention that the results achieved by the expert during sessions with the child, and by the family at home, can be generalized. On the whole, the basic principles explained to parents for managing children with ADHD apply to teachers too, but adapted to the classroom setting. Just as problematic situations arising in the family are observed and analysed, the same can be done at school. Asking teachers to observe a child's behaviour enables the teachers to identify antecedents and consequences of any troublesome behaviour and thus prevent situations that are difficult to manage. Unlike the family environment, the social context created by a child's classmates can have a very important influence on their behaviour in the classroom setting. It is hugely gratifying for any child to be approved by their peers. It is essential to clarify this aspect with teachers and get them to involve the whole class in their intervention, not just the child with ADHD. For instance, children with ADHD often love to make jokes and get people to laugh, but they do not always succeed in doing so at the right time. If they keep interrupting the teacher's lesson, it is important to explain to the whole class how they should behave: if someone makes a joke at an inappropriate time, the children should ignore it instead of laughing.

As we have already said several times, the problems that children with ADHD pose derive from their poor self-regulation, so what parents and teachers should try to do is make their environment as "hetero-regulating" as possible. In other words, these children's environment (in the broadest sense of the term) should be as structured as possible, so that it provides them with useful input concerning how they are expected to behave. A structured and predictable environment makes these children's behaviour easier to control. This can be achieved either by structuring the classroom setting, or by structuring the time and social life in the classroom. Let us see in more detail what we mean by this.

By a structured classroom setting, we mean a place rich in useful information for a child with ADHD. First, we need to consider whether the child is sitting in a place that helps them to concentrate, away from sources of distraction such as a window or door, or classmates with characteristics similar to their own (with whom they are likely to "join forces" to cause trouble). The place where children with ADHD sit in class should facilitate their eye contact with the teacher, and enable the teacher to reach them easily. Even such small adjustments are useful in helping these children to concentrate.

Another very important aspect of the school day for children with ADHD concerns how they manage their time and activities that need to be completed in the classroom. Teachers frequently tell me that, half an hour into the school day, these children are already repeatedly asking how soon it will be playtime. This goes to show how hard it is for them to quantify time. A school day seems to be endless, and often boring, while they wait for the sound of the bell (it is worth recalling Sonuga-Barke's *delay aversion* theory described in Chapter 2). To help these children understand the passage of time, and thus cooperate more in the classroom, we need to try to make time as tangible as possible. For this purpose, it can be useful to structure and schedule every school day. One way to do so would be to write all the activities planned for the day in detail on the blackboard. To give an idea, for the English language lessons, we could write that we will do some reading first, then have some questions on the text we have read (a comprehension test), then do a dictation and then collectively correct our work. We can add an indication of how long each of these activities will take (for smaller children, we could use visual indicators such as arrows of varying length, depending on how long an activity is expected to last), and also of how demanding the task might be (Capodieci & Cester, 2019).

Another element that usually helps children to understand the passage of time is routine. Although it has been mistreated and judged negatively in various settings, in the case of children a routine is very useful because it helps them to know what is going to happen. It should come as no surprise that kindergartens and infant schools have many, clearly identifiable routines; they enable children to understand when the various parts of their day start and end. In the classes of older children too, there are very often routines that may not be explicitly stated, but they are there in the background.

Just as we do with parents, we also explain to teachers that it is very important for children with ADHD to have a clear idea of what behaviour is appropriate in a classroom setting. Instead of repeatedly reminding them of what they are not allowed to do, it is more useful to emphasize (and possibly gratify) their more appropriate behaviour. That is why it helps to identify certain rules that everyone in the class must obey. Most classrooms have a poster somewhere on the wall with a list of behavioural rules, but it should not have a merely decorative purpose. Establishing rules to follow in class serves as a reference concerning how to behave, and everyone – including the teachers – should obey the rules. For children with ADHD, it is best for these rules to be shared, written and as few as possible (about three for younger children, up to five or six for older children) because of their difficulty with handling lots of information at the same time. They should be very clear (short sentences), and presented in a positive format to help children understand what they should do, rather than what they should not do. There should also be clear reinforcements for when they succeed in complying with the rules, and clear consequences for when they fail to do so.

If the rules are based on these recommendations, they usually produce good results. For instance, if the class has a rule that you raise your hand to ask permission to speak, the teacher should only answer children who have raised their hands. If children in the class all start talking at once, the teacher should keep quiet, not answering any of them (and obviously not joining in the shouting to get them all to be quiet) until one child remembers the rule and raises their hand. Then the other children will start to behave in the same way. Rules must be related to the achievement of a goal and, once the desired result has been obtained (i.e. when a given type of behaviour has become a part of daily practice), the rules can also be changed.

Clearly, such methods work well for the whole class, not just for children with ADHD, because their aim is to make the environment more structured, informative and hetero-regulating. Some further steps may be necessary, however, for children with ADHD. For instance, we know that the nature of their disorder makes it impossible for these children to stay seated at their desk for the required amount of time, so the teacher could make a pact with them regarding how to manage their restlessness, which can sometimes become impossible to contain. When a child feels they cannot stay still a moment longer, they can ask the teacher for permission to "stretch their legs" for a minute. This has a dual advantage: it helps the child to understand when they have exhausted their "reserves" and really need to move; and it is a strategy appropriate to the classroom setting, where they must avoid disturbing other people. This strategy can have some advantages for the teachers as well, who can avoid having to interrupt the lesson to rebuke the child for leaving their place without permission.

Another difficult time for children with ADHD is when they have class tests. It can be very hard for them to maintain their concentration for long enough to finish the task, so they may hurry to get the job over and done with. They hand in their paper even though they know they have made some mistakes or not done very well. In this situation it may be useful to divide the test into separate parts. If it involves an essay, for instance, the children with ADHD could be asked to draft their essays in class with the other children, but allowed to copy out their final version at another time or at home.

Dietary measures as a treatment for ADHD

Many parents wonder if there are particular foods that might cause this disorder, and whether modifying their child's diet can lead to some improvement in their symptoms. Below is a brief overview of what we currently know on this matter.

The myth. ADHD is caused by an excessive intake of sugars, preserving agents and other artificial additives in foodstuffs; eliminating these substances from the diet will cure the disorder.

The reality. Numerous studies have shown that very few children have benefited from following any special diet. A lot of research conducted in "double-blind" fashion[1] has ruled out the possibility of sugars and additives being a cause of ADHD (Sonuga-Barke et al., 2013).

A recent systematic literature review (Pelsser, Frankena, Toorman, & Rodrigues Pereira, 2017) of the various studies on the topic indicates that diets lacking in foods containing artificial colouring agents or polyunsaturated fatty acids have very limited effects on the onset of ADHD, so such dietary measures cannot be recommended as a general treatment for the disorder. On the other hand, a diet based on only a few foodstuffs (imagine the sort of diet used in hospitals) can improve some signs and symptoms of the disorder. This justifies the adoption of a *few-foods diet* for diagnostic purposes in subgroups of children with

ADHD who are unresponsive to pharmacological treatment or too young to use it. Further research is needed on the few-foods diet, however, to arrive at a more straightforward diagnostic procedure capable of distinguishing children who respond to this treatment from those who do not. The results of the review conducted in 2017 are in line with the position of the International Society for Nutritional Psychiatry Research; there has recently been some emerging evidence for diet as crucial factor in mental disorders, suggesting that nutrition could become a part of standard diagnostic practice.

Note

1 A clinical trial is defined as double-blind when neither the participants nor the staff conducting the study know which participants are receiving the experimental drug or treatment, and which ones are receiving a placebo.

References

Arnold, L. E., Chuang, S., Davies, M., Abikoff, H. B., Conners, C. K., Elliott, G. R., et al. (2004). Nine months of multicomponent behavioural treatment for ADHD and effectiveness of MTA fading procedures. *Journal of Abnormal Child Psychology, 32*, 39–51.

Bijou, S. W. (1997). *Analisi comportamentale dello sviluppo infantile.* Milano, Italy: McGraw-Hill.

Capodieci, A., & Cester, I. (2019). *Comprendere e gestire il tempo. Potenziare le competenze degli alunni con BES nella scuola primaria [xx].* Trento, Italy: Erickson.

Coghill, D. R., Seth, S., Pedroso, S., Usala, T., Currie, J., & Gagliano, A. (2014). Effects of methylphenidate on cognitive functions in children and adolescents with attention-deficit/hyperactivity disorder: Evidence from a systematic review and a meta-analysis. *Biological Psychiatry, 76(8)*, 603–615.

Cortese, S., Ferrin, M., Brandeis, D., Buitelaar, J., Daley, D., Dittmann, R. W., et al. (2015). Cognitive training for attention-deficit/hyperactivity disorder: Meta-analysis of clinical and neuropsychological outcomes from randomized controlled trials. *Journal of the American Academy of Child & Adolescent Psychiatry, 54(3)*, 164–174.

Cunningham, C. E., Bremner, R., & Boyle, M. (1995). Large group community-based parent training programs for families of preschoolers at risk for disruptive behaviour disorders: Utilization, cost-effectiveness, and outcome. *Journal of Child Psychology and Psychiatry, 36*, 1141–1159.

Eyberg, S. M., Edwards, D., Boggs, S. R., & Foote, R. (1998). Maintaining the treatment effects of parent training: The role of booster sessions and other maintenance strategies. *Clinical Psychology: Science and Practice, 5,* 544–554.

Fabiano, G. A., Chacko, A., Pelham, W. E., Robb, J., Walker, K. S., Wymbs, F., Sastry, A. L. et al. (2009). Comparison of behavioral parent training programs for fathers of children with attention-deficit/hyperactivity disorder. *Behavior Therapy, 40,* 190–204.

Hinshaw, S. P., Owens, E. B., Wells, K. C., Kraemer, H. C., Abikoff, H. B., Arnold, L. E., et al. (2000). Family processes and treatment outcome in the MTA: Negative/ineffective parenting practices in relation to multimodal treatment. *Journal of Abnormal Child Psychology, 28*(6), 555–568.

Jones, K., Daley, D., Hutchings, J., Bywater, T., & Eames, C. (2007). Efficacy of the Incredible Years Basic parent training programme as an early intervention for children with conduct problems and ADHD. *Child: Care, Health and Development, 33*(6), 749–756.

Jones, K., Daley, D., Hutchings, J., Bywater, T., & Eames, C. (2008). Efficacy of the Incredible Years Programme as an early intervention for children with conduct problems and ADHD: Long-term follow-up. *Child: Care, Health and Development, 34*(3), 380–390.

MTA Cooperative Group. (1999a). A 14-month randomized clinical trial of treatment strategies for attention deficit hyperactivity disorder (ADHD). *Archives of General Psychiatry, 56,* 1073–1086.

MTA Cooperative Group. (1999b). Moderators and mediators of treatment response for children with attention-deficit/hyperactivity disorder. *Archives of General Psychiatry, 56,* 1088–1096.

Paiano, A., Re, A. M., Ferruzza, E., & Cornoldi, C. (2014). *Parent Training per l' ADHD. Programma CERG: sostegno, Cognitivo, Emotivo e Relazionale dei genitori [Parent Training for ADHD. CERG Program: support, Cognitive, Emotional and Relational of the parents].* Trento, Italy: Erickson.

Pelsser, L. M., Frankena, K., Toorman, J., & Rodrigues Pereira, R. (2017). Diet and ADHD, reviewing the evidence: A systematic review of meta-analyses of double-blind placebo-controlled trials evaluating the efficacy of diet interventions on the behavior of children with ADHD. *PLoS ONE, 12*(1), e0169277.

Sonuga-Barke, E. J., Brandeis, D., Cortese, S., Daley, D., Ferrin, M., Holtmann, M., et al. (2013). Nonpharmacological interventions for ADHD: Systematic review and meta-analyses of randomized controlled trials of dietary and psychological treatments. *American Journal of Psychiatry, 170,* 275–289.

Swanson, J. M., Arnold, L. E., Vitiello, B., Abikoff, H. B., Wells, K. C., March, J. S., et al. (2002). Response to commentary on the Multimodal

Treatment Study of ADHD (MTA): Mining the meaning of the MTA. *Journal of Abnormal Child Psychology*, 30(4), 327–332.

Tanaka, Y., Rohde, L. A., Feldman, P. D., & Upadhyaya, H. P. (2013). A meta-analysis of the consistency of atomoxetine treatment effects in pediatric patients with attention-deficit/hyperactivity disorder from 15 clinical trials across four geographic regions. *Journal Child and Adolescent Psychopharmacology*, 23(4), 262–270.

Vio, C., Marzocchi, G. M., & Offredi, F. (1999). *Il bambino con Deficit di Attenzione/Iperattività. Diagnosi psicologica e formazione dei genitori.* Trento, Italy: Erickson.

Webster-Stratton, C. (1996). Early Intervention with videotape modeling: Programs for families of children with oppositional defiant disorder or conduct disorder. In E. Hibbs & P. Jensen (Eds.), *Psychosocial treatments for child and adolescent disorders: Empirically based strategies for clinical practice* (pp. 435–474). New York: APA.

Wells, K. C., Epstein, J. N., Hinshaw, S. P., Conners, C. K., Klaric, J., Abikoff, H. B., et al. (2000). Parenting and family stress treatment outcomes in attention deficit hyperactivity disorder (ADHD): An empirical analysis in the MTA study. *Journal of Abnormal Child Psychology*, 28, 543–553.

Chapter 5

Living with ADHD

Practical ways to manage symptoms and consequences

Practical suggestions for managing ADHD symptoms and associated problems

When we meet parents of children or adolescents with ADHD, we often find them very discouraged. They feel they are on their own, struggling to climb a mountain, and they worry that – if they make it to the top – they will only find another, higher mountain up ahead. The anxiety that grips these parents is not entirely unfounded. We have seen how difficult it is to manage children with ADHD, even in their little daily routines. All the problems their parents have to deal with every day mount up, all the negativities escalating, presenting them with a very bleak picture and making them imagine an even more difficult future. Many parents say to me: "If I can't handle him now that he's eight years old, imagine what it'll be like when he's 15!". Simply put, what these parents tend to do is focus on a faraway destination, without envisaging the steps along the way.

In actual fact, what we suggest they do is divide the long-term goals into small stages. This helps them to get things under control, keep anxiety to a minimum and be more productive. The core features of ADHD that have a negative impact on a child's capacity to pursue and achieve goals are inattention, which makes it difficult to focus on a task or specific issue, and impulsivity, which makes these children do whatever crosses their mind and offers instant gratification. In the mind of someone with ADHD, staying clearly and precisely focused on a long-term goal for a period of time is hugely difficult. The characteristics of their disorder are an often insurmountable obstacle to their success, and this has dramatic consequences on their self-esteem and sense of self-efficacy. That is why it is so important to find ways to split the final objective into small, short-term (day-to-day) goals, and to add enticements to keep these children motivated.

A person's sense of self-efficacy (Bandura, 1997) stems from the faith they have in their ability to achieve a given result. It is a variable with an important influence on how well we succeed in achieving one goal, and then setting ourselves new ones for the future.

When we choose goals for children with ADHD, they should be challenging but achievable. They should be specific, practical and measurable, so "doing well at school" is not an appropriate goal, whereas "getting a pass in mathematics" makes it easier to understand whether the goal is achievable or not. Goals should also be *process based*, i.e. they should establish how the process should be organized, and how it can be achieved, step by step. Goals should be set with a precise timing, that should be as realistic as possible. If a child has never got a mark higher than four in mathematics, they can hardly expect to reach a pass mark of six by studying for a week. They need to work in small steps, making small improvements, and hope to arrive at a pass in ten weeks. If the focus is too strongly on the final objective, they may have the impression of never improving enough, so they risk becoming demoralized and giving up. If instead we set small daily goals (e.g. to study maths for 30 minutes) or weekly goals (to get a "star" in maths), and if we compare what the child has done each day with what they had succeeded in doing previously – rather than thinking they still have not reached the final objective – then we can proceed with greater motivation and enthusiasm, increasing the chances of reaching the final goal in the end.

In the following paragraphs, we suggest some strategies for coping with the main problems of ADHD.

How to improve children's ability to focus and maintain their attention for a period of time

When it is time to do homework, it can be helpful to keep children away from sources of distraction (such as mobile phones, televisions, PlayStations and so on), and to set up a specific place where only the materials they need for their studies are to hand. We know that staying concentrated for lengthy periods of time is really difficult for children with ADHD, so it is a good idea to foresee short, but frequent breaks. During these breaks, it is best not to let the child engage in activities that they find particularly activating and stimulating, which would risk distracting them from their studies once and for all. The children should use the breaks to get up and move about, stretch their legs, go to the toilet or have a snack. Playful activities that the children find more pleasant and fun (not sports or group activities) can be used instead as reinforcement when they study more effectively, doing their homework adequately and within the allotted time (Table 5.1). Homework time is often a cause of rows and issues between children and their parents. Children with ADHD will tend to procrastinate, to postpone getting down to work, so it is fundamentally important to help them settle down and concentrate on a given activity for increasingly long periods of time, and offer them a positive reinforcement when they achieve their goal.

Given their hyperactivity and impulsivity, how can we balance the child's need to move with the need to comply with behavioural rules?

We need to create the right conditions to ensure that these children have enough space and to avoid inhibiting their desire to experiment and move around by constantly forbidding and

Table 5.1 Example of a chart for organizing afternoon homework with the method of reinforcement

Behaviour to encourage during afternoon studies (goals)	Tick a box every time the behaviour is adopted (token)					Prize (reinforcement) for getting five ticks
I start doing my homework without being reminded more than three times	X	X				I choose whatever snack I want
I stay concentrated on it for 15 minutes	X	X	X			I can have a five-minute rest
I do all my homework for the next day	X					I can watch an extra 20 minutes of television

criticizing. On the other hand, we need to ensure that they comply with basic behavioural norms. Because of their characteristic impulsiveness, hyperactivity and attention problems, and because these features are frequently associated with a weakness in certain executive functions (Doyle, 2006), children with ADHD have difficulty understanding the consequences of some types of behaviour and how it is most appropriate to behave in a given situation (Box 5.1). Shouting at these children when they make a mistake is not a good solution. In most cases, they do not intend to misbehave. A lack of clear and simple rules that the children have properly understood and learned, a weak motivation to follow them and the sense of immediate gratification they experience on doing what crosses their mind (or even merely desiring to do so) straight away combine to make these children do something wrong even before they themselves or the people around them realize! This elicits a scolding, which arrives like a bolt from the blue. It makes them feel frustrated and guilty without clearly understanding why. They do not know how to redress the situation, and they can tell that they have disappointed their parents yet again. It is easy to see that, in the long run, this sense of frustration without a chance to discuss and understand their mistakes generates a sense of anger. Faced with yet another rebuke, the children may react aggressively, and this triggers a vicious cycle in which everybody loses. That is why it is so essential to help these children grasp the positive and negative consequences of their actions, not only in the case of the

---

Box 5.1 "What if ..."

A simple and fun way to help children to understand can be to get members of the family to play a game called *What if ... ?* It consists in taking turns to answer a question in whatever way we wish. The questions could range from "What if I go down the stairs three steps at the time?", "What if I swing on my chair?", for instance, to questions concerning aspects of social interaction (which is impaired in individuals with ADHD), such as "What if I take one of your toys without asking?", "What if you speak to me and I don't listen?", "What if you interrupt me when I'm speaking?" and so on.

more "extreme" episodes, but also in all those daily situations that are a cause of concern for others.

It is also essential to explain clearly to children with ADHD what they *can* do, rather than what they cannot do, so that they understand what behaviour is expected of them, and how they might try to adopt it. Generally speaking, it is advisable not to give them too much information or too many instructions at once. This is because one of the executive functions that is most impaired in ADHD is working memory, which is the ability to both retain information in the mind and succeed in working on it. It is best to establish a few straightforward rules to help the child understand how they must behave in various settings and at various times of day. For the same reasons, it is also a good idea to reinforce any positive behaviour the child engages in. Simply put, this means making sure that there are more frequent opportunities for this behaviour, so that the association between the desired behaviour and the context in which it occurs is strengthened (Box 5.2).

It is common, however, for parents to be upset and disappointed when their child misbehaves or fails to do what is expected of them. When this happens, they are likely to forget to mention what the child did well instead. But it is always very important to reinforce the child's self-esteem by congratulating

---

Box 5.2 Reinforcement

One question that parents of children with ADHD often ask is about the method of reinforcements and consequences: "Will I have to go on reinforcing him for life just to get him to do as I ask? Then he'll never do anything unless I give him something in exchange!"

As explained earlier, this method is used as a facilitation for children with ADHD whose particular characteristics make it hard for them to interiorize an adult hetero-control and gain sufficient self-control over what they do. Reinforcements and consequences are not for always. Quite the reverse: the sooner functional strategies are identified and followed, the sooner the child will succeed in interiorizing them and achieving a degree of self-control.

them for even the smallest successes, for kind gestures and for everything about them that can be appreciated. It is essential to emphasize their strengths, even though we sometimes unfortunately struggle to notice them.

Why do I always seem to be in a hurry, and constantly late, with my child? Why do we seem to try twice as hard as everyone else but never get good results?

Another core aspect of managing children and adolescents with ADHD concerns the need to be organized and take a systematic approach to reaching our established goals. The various activities that children engage in during the day must be scheduled in the best possible way, always specifying what time they start and end. It can be helpful to use a calendar, displayed somewhere at home where it is clearly visible, and to mark it with images or words (depending on the child's age) so that the programme for each day of the week is clear. We can include the school timetable, sporting commitments and any other kind of routine activity, using stickers for additional activities or occasional appointments that may be arranged from time to time. It can also be useful to set a time, such as Sunday evenings, when parents can check the calendar together with their child, reminding them of what is on during the coming week, and making a note together about any extra activities or changes to the usual weekly programme. It is important not to suddenly change the daily schedule without informing the child.

As we saw in Chapter 2, researchers have shown that children with ADHD have difficulty in certain executive functions, which are complex mental capabilities that – among other things – enable us to plan and organize our activities (Abikoff & Gallagher, 2008). They also have shortcomings in estimating and managing matters of time (Castellanos & Tannock, 2002). That is why it is important to help these children devise strategies and methods to compensate for these difficulties. Aids such as calendars, diaries and checklists can help these children to live more serenely and with a greater sense of well-being. So, we should help them to organize their schoolwork, for instance: they could distinguish their school subjects by colour, make a checklist of the materials needed for each subject, plan their studies for the week and check whether they have done all their homework (which must be done with the help of an adult in some cases). Very often it is enough for an adult to be present and to serve as an external regulator, without taking any direct part in actually doing the work. Young children rely entirely on adults to manage their school commitments, but as they grow older they develop the ability to cope with things alone. This process is rather more difficult for children with ADHD: when they reach an age at which parents would normally expect them to remember their schoolbooks, their homework and their deadlines, this does not happen – and they are often scolded as a result. These children need help, right from when they are very small, to learn strategies that make it easier for them to organize and remember what they have to do, and what materials they need. Involving them and explaining how to use various planning aids will facilitate their passage towards independence. It also prevents them from constantly feeling they may have forgotten something, or worrying about having got the day of an appointment wrong. When things do not go according to plan, parents should try to see the situation as an opportunity: it can be used as an experience that helps the child to grow up, and as a chance to discuss what went wrong with the strategies adopted and what remedy to use to avoid the situation cropping up again.

To help children not to lose control of the situation, there are also a few tricks to bear in mind. These tricks enable them to deal more serenely with daily life or new situations, such as a school trip or a family holiday.

A first aspect consists in organizing well-structured situations. To avoid children with ADHD finding themselves unprepared and feeling they do not know how to deal with a situation, or reacting hyperactively or impulsively, it is important to use routines that make situations predictable, as explained in the case of structuring the school day. In addition to a calendar of daily activities, it can be useful to prepare posters illustrating the series of actions needed when they wake up (a time of day when parents may be in a hurry, and easily become angry if their child does not do as they are told). A list of activities in sequential order and a set of times (constructed using pictures in the case of smaller children) can prove extremely helpful and start the day on the right note. Here is an example (adaptable to the family's habits and the features of its members):

7.00 Mum comes into my room and raises the blind;
7.05 I get up and go and have a wee;
7.08 I go to the kitchen for breakfast;
7.20 I wash my face and clean my teeth;
7.25 I get dressed;
7.35 I put on my shoes;
7.40 we leave the house.

It could be worth drawing up a similar list for the evenings and for bedtime (which children with ADHD tend to try and postpone).

20.00 we all have dinner together;
20.30 I put my plate, cutlery and glass on the kitchen worktop;
20.35 I get my school bag ready, making sure I have everything I need for the next day;
20.45 we switch on the TV;
21.15 I get into my pyjamas and clean my teeth;
21.25 I get under the bedcovers;
21.30 I say good night and switch off the light.

Children with ADHD struggle to follow such a schedule, so a system of reinforcements and consequences can be useful – especially at the start – to increase their motivation to try. For instance, we can agree that, if they keep to the schedule, they can choose what programme to watch on television next day. On the other hand, if they do not keep to the schedule, they will only be able to watch half as much television next day. Here again, the reinforcements and consequences depend on the age and abilities of the child concerned.

As well as organizing structured situations, it is hugely important to help these children learn to be tidy. They can be given small tasks to complete that are suited to their age and capabilities (such as tidying up their school materials, their toys and so on). We need to remember that we must always choose realistic, specific goals that can be achieved within a short time span and that are challenging but achievable. We should provide reinforcement, congratulating the children when they succeed in doing as they were asked.

Given these children's tendency to be untidy and disorganized, we routinely need to check their school diary (in case teachers have left notes the children have forgotten to mention) and school materials (to make sure they have not lost anything). While doing so, we should teach them to check for themselves, helping them to become increasingly independent. Together we can use the checklists of school materials we prepared to remind them what to take to school each day to check the contents of their school bag at the end of the week. We need to see whether they still have everything they had taken to school so that they can bring home anything they have forgotten. It can help to have a clearly defined place at home where their school things should be put, as this makes it easier to see if anything is missing. It is also a good idea to help these children tidy their desk or wardrobe based on a few simple criteria (e.g. arranging their jumpers or other clothing by colour, dividing their stationery by type and so on, see Box 5.3).

Box 5.3 Tidying the room

How do we help adolescents with ADHD tidy their room? Is the situation out of control by now, with only patches of floor still visible? After asking them for months to tidy up, did you decide to ignore their room, but now they cannot find the technical drawings they did last year?

Try to keep calm, take a deep breath and let us see if we can find a way to help them, also with a view to the times when they will be away from home to study or go on holiday with friends. First of all, parents should remind their children that being "physically" tidy and "mentally" tidy amounts to the same thing; helping them to keep their space tidy is an important way to help children and adolescents with ADHD. Of course, your child's motivation to be tidy will be minimal, but you can try to make it look more like a game and, if necessary (and it probably will be), resort to using a system of reinforcements and consequences.

A first useful thing to do is to get the child to "classify" the objects in the room as things "to keep", "to bin" or "to give away". They can also use colours to distinguish between the three categories and attach stickers of the appropriate colour. It is best to use a timer to avoid spending more than a couple of minutes on each item to be classified. If no decision has been reached when the time is up, then the object can be binned. This job can be done for half an hour at a time, with approximately ten-minute breaks. Once everything has been separated, it will be necessary to get rid of the items to be binned or given away as promptly as possible. For the objects being kept, it is necessary to establish whether they can be put away or need to be to hand because they are used every day. To do so, the same method can be used as in the previous selection process.

Then suitable places need to be found for the objects to keep, but put away. Finally, containers can be used for the items in everyday use, with a system of labels that make it easier to always know where to find things, and so that they do not get mislaid. For instance, there could be three such containers, one in the hall for mobile phones, one in the kitchen for house keys and one in the bedroom for purses and wallets. These objects should only be placed in their various containers and never anywhere else. If it is hard to know where to start, the room can be divided into several zones and tidied one zone at a time, with reinforcements available for each zone completed. Then it can be useful to take "before and after" photographs to document the progress children make, and motivate them to keep things tidy in future.

Technology

A classic question that parents of children and adolescents with ADHD ask regards their use of television, mobile phones and video games. *They would spend all day on the phone, or at the PlayStation. What should we do? We ask them to switch it off, but they refuse. How should we react? How long is it okay for them to use these things?* It would be impossible these days to exclude mobile phones and electronic games from the life of the young, and even the very young (12% of under-17-year-olds who possess a mobile phone are less than ten years old), but it is fundamentally important to establish rules concerning their use. Adolescents are hyper-connected nowadays, but it is a good idea to bear in mind some guidelines. It would be best not to give them a mobile phone before they are 13 years old (though this suggestion is now increasingly ignored). Between the ages of 11 and 17, they should not spend more than three hours a day using their mobile phones. Research has established that using them for more than five hours a day causes problems with sleeping and school-work, and is associated with a more limited learning capacity and irritability – all alarm bells for the onset of a form of dependence. Nor should we underestimate eyesight problems and a tendency to become overweight as a result of eating more and unhealthily, as happens in those who use their mobile phones at mealtimes. For both mobile phones and online games, there is also a risk of social isolation, with young people becoming reclusive, living online and avoiding the real world (Stip, Thibault, Beauchamp-Chatel, & Kisely, 2016). Naturally, it is essential for parents to give a good example (as in other aspects of their children's upbringing) because children copy their parents' behaviour. If the adults are the first to be constantly checking their mobile phones, they can hardly expect their children to do otherwise. Mobile phones are also often used by parents as an "anti-anxiety strategy", to check on where their child is and who they are with. Finally, it is important for parents to be informed not only about their child's real life, but also about their "digital life", what activities they engage in online, what games they love to play and how they work (Lavenia, 2012).

Schooling problems: strategies for studying at home and in class

Students with ADHD are just as bright and intelligent as their peers, but usually have lower school marks. They are much more likely to fail in exams, and much more likely to leave school at an early age (Barkley, 2013).

When we ask students with ADHD to describe how they learn and the strategies they use when taking tests, we find that – by comparison with students without ADHD – they encounter difficulties in eight out of ten of the areas investigated that are important to academic success (Levrini & Prevatt, 2012).

Here in detail are the main issues they characteristically experience.

Concentration. It is hardly surprising that students with ADHD should have problems concentrating. Their mind wanders while they are studying; they fail to listen carefully in class; they tend to think about other things during lessons; and once they have lost their concentration they struggle to regain it.

Time management. Students with ADHD tend to procrastinate and then find themselves studying for tests at the last minute. They find it hard to establish a daily study plan and, even when they do, they are very often unable to keep to it.

Integrating information. Students with ADHD are not in the habit of using strategies that help them make connections and fully understand the concepts they are studying, whereas their peers without ADHD try to correlate what they are studying with what they already know, making logical associations and saying things in their own words to make them easier to understand.

Self-testing. Students with ADHD tend to use fewer strategies, such as rereading notes they made during the lessons before they take a test, or asking themselves possible questions to help their learning process.

Identifying core ideas. Students with ADHD have trouble identifying the important information during lessons or in what they read. They tend to get lost in the details and to lose sight of the general idea.

Strategies for use in tests. Students with ADHD are not very good at preparing for tests. They report not being good at studying in general and not knowing how to adapt their study methods to suit a given type of test. They say that studying takes up a lot of their time. They usually do worse in tests than in ordinary lessons – even when they have studied enough and know the important information – because they often do not read the instructions properly and do not check their work.

Motivation. Students with ADHD have difficulty staying motivated when they come up against particular topics or school subjects that they do not find very interesting. They struggle to motivate themselves, and it is easy for them to abandon activities when they become complicated.

Anxiety. Students with ADHD report that, whether they are studying or taking a test, they feel very anxious and worry they will make mistakes.

There are two areas, however, where students with ADHD are on a par with students without the disorder, and these concern asking for help with their studies and their attitude to school. In fact, they tend to use services for supporting students in their studies more frequently than students without ADHD. They also ask their parents for help or ask classmates to help them check their work, and they talk to teachers about their difficulties. As concerns their attitude to school, we have seen that students with ADHD have just as much interest in learning as their classmates, and – though their motivation may sometimes be in short supply – their approach to their education is generally very positive.

As already mentioned, one fundamental aspect that negatively influences the academic performance of young people with ADHD is self-regulation, i.e. the set of abilities that, combined together, enable people to control and modify their own behaviour. When students have a limited capacity for self-regulation, they are penalized in various ways: they have difficulty taking notes, paying attention during lessons, studying a text and writing a précis or essay, and they perform poorly in tests. Students with ADHD have more difficulty summarizing or gleaning the most important information from a text because they very often forget what they have just learned. Or they focus on details because the general gist tends to escape them, and they soon become demotivated and give up when the difficulty of a task increases. Their problem lies not so much in not knowing how to do their school work, but rather in the difficulty of regulating themselves while doing so. We discuss certain capabilities that can help with these issues (see Box 5.4).

Box 5.4 How to improve children's ability to study

Below is a list of practical suggestions that can help to make it easier for young people with ADHD to study.

- Spending hours and hours on books is not a good idea for children and adolescents with ADHD. It is better to study for periods of time lasting between 20 and 50 minutes, separated by breaks of 5–10 minutes.
- It is crucial to have an environment conducive to study. It is easy to guess that situations where children or adolescents with ADHD might become distracted should be avoided. Switch off the television, mobile phones and game consoles for the time it takes them to study or do their homework.

- Begin with the more difficult school subjects or activities so that, when they start getting tired or bored, or want to stop, they will be gratified by switching to easier tasks.
- Make sure they have a clear idea of what they have to do, and fully understand what they have to study in order to use the time usefully, doing nothing that could subsequently prove pointless.
- Make sure they have a comfortable chair and desk. Do not let them study in bed. Beds are for sleeping and chairs are for studying. It is important not to confuse the body's needs. This also helps to prevent sleep disorders (as discussed in Chapter 3).
- Get them into the habit of doing something every day. Even spending just half an hour a day on schoolwork helps to avoid them procrastinating, and then having to study or do exercises at the last minute before a test. If they do a little every day, at the end of the week they will feel they have achieved something, and will feel gratified and reinforced.
- Provide small rewards for every half an hour of study (snacks, stickers), and a larger one at the end of the week (swimming pool or cinema).
- Facilitate opportunities for them to study with their classmates (preferably one at a time to start with), as this can be more fun and motivating. It is naturally important to choose the right type of classmate – preferably one who has a positive attitude to school and their studies, and who can teach the child something about the strategies they use to study more effectively.

In an interesting study conducted at the University of North Texas (Kaminski, Turnock, Rosén, & Laster, 2006), researchers asked students with ADHD what helped them to be successful at school. The things they mentioned were: first, working longer and harder than anyone else; second, making use of social support, e.g. asking parents, friends and teachers for help; third, using good strategies to manage their time; fourth, practising a lot; and last, but no less important, having a positive mental attitude to their school work.

Right from when children with ADHD start primary school, it is important to help them experience their school life as fun, to arouse their curiosity and thereby promote their motivation to learn.

Suggestions for the abilities needed in secondary school

> I try hard in class. I feel motivated and think I can manage. But then, when I reread the notes I've taken, I can't understand a thing. Sometimes, while I'm taking them I realize I've fallen behind, so I give up.

This is the sort of thing we often hear from students with ADHD in secondary school. In fact, it is quite common for many children with ADHD to cope with the study demands of primary school with no particular difficulties, even if their results are not particularly good. This is partly because they have fewer teachers, and it is often easier for these teachers to create a supportive network and devise strategies suitable for each of their pupils. When children with ADHD move on to secondary school, many of them experience a marked decline in their academic performance. The study demands increase. They need to take notes. There are far more different teachers, and sometimes the amount of work to be done means that it is the students who have to adapt to a teacher's methods rather than the other way around. In light of all these considerations, we provide a few suggestions regarding the specific abilities needed to study, especially from secondary school onwards.

Taking notes

It is important to help adolescents with ADHD to become organized. They need to have an exercise book for each school subject, or a large ring binder with loose sheets that they can arrange by topic. If the second option seems best, it is a good idea to get them into the habit of always writing the date and topic at the top of the sheet of paper – then, if they get the sheets mixed up, they will know straight away how to put them in order. They can write their notes on the main part of the page, using single key words or phrases (given that ADHD is associated with working memory difficulties, it is hard for these students to listen to what is being said and write it down at the same time). It can be useful to use abbreviations and symbols. Straight after the lesson (or as soon as possible), it is important to urge them to reread their notes so that they can complete any information that is not clear or missing while what they studied is still fresh in their memory. The right-hand side of the page could have a column for any questions to ask the teacher. When studying independently, they can try to answer these questions themselves, preferably aloud, so as to commit the information to their long-term memory. When they are repeating and revising, it is also helpful for them to try to connect new information with what they already know, or with practical aspects and life experiences.

Reading a text

> At some point, even if I'm reading aloud, my mind begins to wander, following up some idea triggered by a word in the text. Then I no longer know what I was reading, and up to what point I had been paying attention. I've even tried using audiobooks – starting with Harry Potter because I really enjoyed the film – but it was even worse. In the end I was falling asleep ...

This is how Matthew, a 12-year-old with ADHD, explains his experience of reading. But studying necessarily involves reading and, in some cases, students need to read several passages or even whole books in order to complete a school assignment. Below are some suggested strategies to help adolescents with ADHD in this type of learning situation.

The first things we suggest are activities to train their concentration – an ability fundamental to reading and studying successfully. We can advise them to pay attention to when they start to become distracted, and to make a conscious effort to ignore the distraction. This strategy needs to be learned, of course, but it can be helpful in numerous settings. Another useful trick is for them to add an asterisk at the end of any sentence they have not really been focusing on, and only proceed with their reading if they are sure they have concentrated on the last sentence they read from start to finish. Every time they notice their mind has begun to wander, they need to go back and concentrate on the last sentence they recall – even trying to visualize what they had read in their mind's eye. It is best not to try to get them to read too much in one go, but to let them switch activity instead. For instance, if they have managed to stay concentrated on their reading for 15–20 minutes, it is better to stop there and do something else (such as maths exercises), before going back to the text. If it is clear that they are becoming too tired, it is a good idea to suggest they go and wash their face, have a drink or do some breathing exercises before starting again.

If these youngsters with ADHD tend to be distracted by certain thoughts, advise them to take a sheet of paper and write the thoughts down so that they can go back to them later when they have finished studying. You can also set aside a time in the day when you can spend ten minutes talking about these intrusive thoughts that cropped up while they were studying.

To improve their ability to read for their studies, we recommend they do so more actively, by taking notes while they are reading and jotting down possible questions, rather than passively reading the same passage several times. Another way is to stop at the end of each paragraph and ask them to say out loud what the paragraph was about, to avoid them discovering after several pages that they are unsure about the content. In some cases, and depending on the students' learning style, it may be useful to use sketches, draw maps or associate what they read with images.

Memory strategies

Researchers tell us that students with ADHD very often have recall problems, particularly as concerns their working memory, because of its link with attentional aspects (Martinussen, Hayden, Hogg-Johnson, & Tannock, 2005). In fact, we need to pay a great deal of attention in order to keep several pieces of information in mind and also manipulate them at the same time. Here are some useful suggestions to help young people with ADHD when, during the course of their school careers, they are faced with the need to commit a lot of information to memory.

First of all, it is a good idea to remember that before asking a child to memorize a concept, we need to make sure they have understood it. For all those bits of information that have to be stored in our memory just as they are (dates, names, places, formulas etc.), we can use flashcards that children can keep with them to look at when they have a minute to spare. Whenever possible, it is also useful to draw pictures, sketches or maps of what they need to learn, or to get the learner to imagine moving along a route they know well, and place items of information that are difficult to memorize along the way (the method of loci, Groninger, 1971). Another useful trick is to use mnemonic to remember lists of words that make up a sentence, such as: A Good Old Boy Always Loves His Momma to remember Aluminium, Gold, Oxygen, Boron, Arsenic, Lithium, Hydrogen and Magnesium. Numbers or important dates can also be used to keep in mind altitudes, distances or historical events.

Writing an essay or a report

Children and adolescents with ADHD very often struggle with writing on various levels, i.e. text production, spelling and handwriting (see Chapter 1). This issue is also associated with the trouble they have taking notes and understanding what they have written. Their spelling tends to get worse when they are more tired and their cognitive resources decline, but it can be kept under control by conducting an effective check on what they have produced. As for the production of a written text, a highly complex activity that also demands various mental functions such as planning, memory and attention, we can offer some practical suggestions. It is best to start with the title chosen by the students or their teachers to get an idea of what they have to talk about. Then it is useful for them to write a list of bullet points with the information they plan to include or the topics they want to deal with. Next, they need to try and arrange these items of information, grouping them by topic or arranging them into sections and subsections. Then they can jot down some notes containing the information they want to include in each section, and subsequently develop it with more descriptive details. It helps to remind them that a text is easier to understand and appealing to read if each sentence contains a single idea or concept, and the sentences are kept short. Last, but not least, they need to reread and correct their work. This phase is fundamentally important, especially for students with ADHD, because it enables them to correct spelling mistakes, repetitions and omissions. They can also rearrange sentences that are complicated or unclear, and see if their text has covered all the necessary aspects. It is important to get them into the habit – right from an early age – of checking their work. Some special time should be spent on this activity, and reinforcement should be offered every time they succeed in going over what they have written. A little trick that can help them pick up on their spelling mistakes or typos is to reread their text "crabwise", i.e. reading all the words working backwards from the end. This obliges them to read each single word more carefully, without relying on its context (Re, Cazzaniga, Pedron, Cornoldi, 2009).

Taking tests

For students with ADHD to succeed in a test and demonstrate what they have learned, it is important for them to arrive on time in class and to take all the time they need to prepare their materials. They should be advised to ask the teachers to let them sit where they are not easily distracted by the surrounding environment or their classmates (and therefore preferably in the front row). When they are given their test paper, it is essential that they follow certain instructions precisely, i.e. do not start straight away; first read everything slowly and carefully; make sure they have everything they need; think carefully about how best to proceed to answer the questions or complete the test; and then – and only then – put pen to paper. The impulsivity typical of students with ADHD can severely penalize them in test situations, especially if they encounter one exercise where they are asked to tick true claims, followed by one where they have to tick false ones, for instance. Because of the features of ADHD, if students with the disorder do not follow the sort of suggestions outlined above, they will continue to tick the true claims, and consequently get all of the second exercise wrong. So, their test result will not reflect how effectively they had studied. It will simply punish them for acting impulsively and not paying enough attention to the instructions. But getting a bad mark after studying hard is not going to have a reinforcing effect and motivate these young people to study more. Quite the reverse. It will make them want to give up and throw in the sponge.

Another useful approach to tests for these students is to start with the easier questions. This helps them to feel more calm and surer of themselves before they deal with the harder questions. It is also useful for them to have a watch so that they can see how much time they have available to complete the test, while still leaving a few minutes to spare at the end to reread the instructions and check their work. They should also try hard to write tidily because, however correct their answers may be, handing in a test paper that is a mess is bound to make a less favourable impression on the teacher.

Anxiety

Many children and adolescents with ADHD, especially when they reach secondary school, can develop severe levels of anxiety, which further worsens their school performance. Getting numerous bad marks, even when they were sure they had studied and done well, makes them very apprehensive about tests. They worry they will fail and be a disappointment to others. If such a situation develops, it is important to find a qualified professional or person with expertise in these matters who can help them to cope. The specialist will focus mainly on the pointless negative thoughts that feed their anxiety, and on cognitive and behavioural strategies they can use to keep calm. These may include breathing exercises; identifying pointless negative thoughts and replacing them with more useful, realistic ones; and asking teachers to help them create more facilitating conditions (relating, for instance, to where they sit in class, keeping their desk uncluttered, having classmates sitting nearby who help them to concentrate).

Generally speaking, we feel that – by adopting appropriate strategies both at home and at school, and right from the start of their school careers – the level of anxiety experienced by children with ADHD can be minimized. If they have the impression of being well-organized, of having prepared adequately for each day, of having the situation under control and not being at the mercy of events, and if they know they can count on the understanding of their parents and teachers, all this helps them to avoid becoming over-anxious. Then they should only experience an appropriate amount of apprehension for tests and school work, which is natural and useful for motivating every student to do their best (the Yerkes-Dodson curve, 1908).

ADHD and physical exercise

Certainly, one of the topics that emerges most frequently with parents when talking about children with ADHD is sport. *What sports could they practice? Are group sports or individual sports best? The child has already tried lots of sports, but soon tired of them and wanted to change.*

It is well known and a commonly shared experience that sports are beneficial on a physical and psychological level. Sports can be a very positive factor in the treatment of children with ADHD for the simple reason that they usually feel less left out by their peers, and less exposed to the risk of a loss of self-esteem when they are practising sports. The abilities required in the school classroom are at odds with the characteristics of their disorder, but in sports they can often do well and find a gratifying environment.

Deciding the best sport for a child with ADHD is not always easy because the choice should be based on a delicate balance of factors, including the nature of the disorder, the child's particular features, the characteristics of the sport and the organizational, economic and emotional needs of the child's parents. It is best to avoid sports that are very chaotic, and those in which it is difficult to decode the setting in order to adopt the expected behaviour (as might be the case in baseball, for instance). It is preferable to choose individual or group sports with very simple rules, clearly limited spaces and set plays that are not constantly changing on the basis of agreements between the players. Finally, success should not be measured mainly on the strength of the players' social interaction skills. An appropriate sport can help children with ADHD to improve their social skills, but some sports may have the opposite effect. For instance, a team sport where there is a lot of competition even among players on the same side could worsen the already delicate balance of children with the typical traits of ADHD.

Then there are some more individual variables to consider before choosing a sport. It is important:

- to consider the child's real motor skills: if their muscle tone is weak, and they find motor coordination difficult, they are better suited to sports such as swimming, dancing, trekking, horse riding, martial arts and cycling, because they do not demand a great degree of physical fitness to start with. This enables the child to use their own physical capabilities, strength, flexibility and coordination, improving their performance over time;

• to see if a child is particularly resistant to engaging in competitive situations: if so, we need to consider a sport with a limited competitive element, or start with an individual sport. There are plenty of activities that do not demand a competitive spirit: trekking, mountain biking, yoga, dancing, fishing and golf are good examples;

• to consider whether the child seems very unwilling to take part in group sports: in this case, we could choose an activity that has all the appearances of an individual sport, but actually has group-related connotations; a sport that enables the child to participate without needing to interpret the verbal signals coming from others, such as team swimming, archery, athletics, bowling, fencing, wrestling, cycling and sailing.

Another aspect that it is useful to bear in mind is that it may be preferable to choose a sport that involves plenty of movement (e.g. football, rugby, basketball), rather than a sport that necessarily includes periods of inactivity, possibly associated with the need to concentrate (obvious examples are baseball or golf).

Whatever the choice of sport, it is important to encourage these children, listen when they talk about their interests and try to go along with them as much as possible if they seem keen to practice a given sport.

A good case to mention on this issue is Lawrence, an eight-year-old boy with severe ADHD and major difficulties at school and with his classmates. When in class, he is unable to stay seated at his desk for more than 15 minutes at a time. He does not listen to the teachers. He is isolated by the other children in class because of the way he behaves towards them. Lawrence is very physical and impetuous. He is tall for his age and really keen on doing well at school. Given his difficulties, he tends to be disruptive and his classmates consequently find him a problem. Lawrence has been playing rugby for three years now. His trainer describes him as motivated and very capable, and he has a strong bond with his teammates. He is attentive and complies strictly with the captain's instructions. Feeling appreciated and capable, he is happier with these companions and in this environment, where his self-esteem is at least partially intact.

Another word on the martial arts, which are often recommended because of their attention to order and discipline. There are some aspects to consider, partly depending on the child's age, the severity of their ADHD and their motivation. When martial arts are taught to children in the early years of their schooling, they contain no violent element and they have the advantage of being a group sport. The children are taught to go through certain motions with a set timing. But it can be frustrating for a child with severe ADHD to see that they are unable to do what the others are doing, and if this happens the whole point of doing sport as an opportunity for gratification and to boost the child's self-esteem would be lost. Finally, the characteristics of these disciplines are sometimes in contrast with the traits of ADHD, so it is important for the children involved to be genuinely motivated. They must be interested in these activities and enjoy themselves, rather than merely submitting to something imposed by their parents.

For children with ADHD, sports are a good idea. Parents should approach them with enthusiasm, and with the necessary awareness that sports can have a beneficial effect on their child's treatment as the social inclusion they entail can help their child to become socially more integrated and also learn to manage their disorder better.

References

Abikoff H., Gallagher R. (2008) Assessment and remediation of organizational skills deficits in children with ADHD. In: K. McBurnett & L. Pfiffner (Eds). *Attention Deficit Hyperactivity Disorder: Concepts, controversies, new directions* (pp. 137–152). New York, NY: Informa Healthcare USA.

Bandura, A. (1997). *Autoefficacia: teoria e applicazioni [Self-efficacy: Theory and applications]*. Trento, Italy: Erikson.

Barkley, R. A. (2013). *Taking charge of ADHD: The complete, authoritative guide for parents*. New York, NY: Guilford press.

Castellanos, F. X., & Tannock, R. (2002). Neuroscience of attention-deficit/hyperactivity disorder: The search for endophenotypes. *Nature Reviews Neuroscience, 3*(8), 617.

Doyle, A. E. (2006). Executive functions in attention-deficit/hyperactivity disorder. *The Journal of Clinical Psychiatry, 67*, 21–26.

Groninger, L. D. (1971). Mnemonic imagery and forgetting. *Psychonomic Science, 23*, 161–163.

Kaminski, P. L., Turnock, P. M., Rosén, L. A., & Laster, S. A. (2006). Predictors of academic success among college students with attention disorders. *Journal of College Counseling, 9*(1), 60–71.

Lavenia, G. (2012). *Internet e le sue dipendenze: dal coinvolgimento alla psicopatologia.* Milano, Italy: FrancoAngeli.

Levrini, A., & Prevatt, F. (2012). *Succeeding with adult ADHD: Daily strategies to help you achieve your goals and manage your life.* Washington, DC: American Psychological Association.

Martinussen, R., Hayden, J., Hogg-Johnson, S., & Tannock, R. (2005). A meta-analysis of working memory impairments in children with attention-deficit/hyperactivity disorder. *Journal of the American Academy of Child & Adolescent Psychiatry, 44*(4), 377–384.

Re, A. M., Cazzaniga, S., Pedron, M., & Cornoldi, C. (2009). *Io scrivo: valutazione e potenziamento delle abilità di espressione scritta [I wrote: Assessment and empowerment of expressive writing skills].* Firenze, Italy: Giunti OS.

Stip, E., Thibault, A., Beauchamp-Chatel, A., & Kisely, S. (2016). Internet addiction, hikikomori syndrome, and the prodromal phase of psychosis. *Frontiers in Psychiatry, 7,* 6.

Yerkes, R. M., & Dodson, J. D. (1908). The relation of strength of stimulus to rapidity of habit formation. *Journal of Comparative Neurology and Psychology, 18*(5), 459–482.

Chapter 6

Managing social difficulties and communicating the diagnosis to peers

Introduction

As emerged several times in previous chapters, young people with ADHD have features related to their disorder that give rise to problems in their relations and communication with parents, siblings, teachers, classmates and friends.

In this chapter, we provide some suggestions on how to help children with ADHD improve their social and communication skills in order to have better relations with their peers and with their teachers. If they are more cooperative, their teachers will be better able to adopt appropriate teaching methods to help them develop their social skills as well as their academic abilities.

According to researchers, approximately 50–60% of children with ADHD have trouble making and keeping friends, and most of them are also unaware of their limited social competence (Dendy, 2011). Children with ADHD tend to have problematic, inconsistent and short-lived social relations and, in the long term, this can have negative consequences, even leading to severe behavioural and/or emotional issues (Bagwell, Molina, Pelham, & Hoza, 2001). In other words, adolescents with ADHD who have had difficult relationships with their peers in childhood are at higher risk of criminal behaviour, depression and substance use than young people with the disorder who did not have trouble socializing with other children (Greene, Biederman, Faraone, Sienna, & Garcia-Jetton, 1997). One study on girls with ADHD showed that being rejected by their peers in childhood was a significant predictor of poor academic results, destructive behaviour, anxiety and depression in adolescence (Mikami & Hinshaw, 2006).

That is why we dedicate a specific chapter to the social problems associated with ADHD and strategies for managing them, describing a few useful tools that can make it easier for young people with this disorder to manage their social relations at home and at school.

Managing the social difficulties of children with ADHD in the family

Let us imagine we are dealing with one of the children described in this book and, with a professional's help, we want to see what it is most important to do for them.

Helping them to manage their aggressiveness and use appropriate strategies to cope with their negative feelings and strong emotions

As mentioned previously, children with ADHD tend to be scarcely aware of their particular characteristics, as concerns both their disruptive behaviour and their way of relating to others. That is why they fail to understand their classmates' reactions towards them when they do something wrong. They consequently feel hurt, and see the others' behaviour as disrespectful and deliberately unkind. This triggers their negative reaction and a sort of vicious cycle sets in. On the other hand, their classmates are often overwhelmed by the energy and liveliness of children with ADHD, and this makes them react badly. They become impatient with these children's inability to play by the rules and their constant need for social reinforcement and gratification (they always want to win, for instance), and all these factors make it difficult to include them in any activity. Both at home and at school it can be useful to suggest to children with ADHD to try and imagine themselves in the place of their classmates. We need to help them understand what makes people behave in certain ways. It is always rather startling for people who do not have the disorder to see how children with ADHD react when they are rebuked for their disruptive behaviour. They seem genuinely surprised, and clearly find it difficult to change their attitude, which can be rather irritating. This is because, as we mentioned in Chapter 3, there is an automatic element in their behaviour that prevents them from being fully aware of what they are doing. Take the example of when children keep interrupting when their parents are talking to each other; one of the parents may stop and say: "I'm talking to your mummy/daddy. You shouldn't interrupt" (rather than just saying "Be quiet a minute", which does not help the children to understand what they have done wrong). When they interrupt again, the parent might say: "I'm talking to your mummy/daddy. You shouldn't interrupt. If you do, I can't finish what I have to say". On the third interruption, they could say: "I'm talking to your mummy/daddy. Just keep in mind what you want to say and, as soon as we've finished, you can tell us". Having to say all this every time, instead of just saying "That's enough!" is obviously tiring and difficult, but, little by little, it will enable these children to become more aware of their behaviour, and to decipher social situations more effectively.

As children with ADHD grow up, we can explain certain social situations to them, getting them to understand how they themselves behave and what is expected of them. It can be useful to ask them what they think might have been wrong in what they were doing, and what it might be more useful and appropriate to do instead. To give an example, if during dinner they leave the table to go and do something else, we can ask them to think about why such behaviour is socially inappropriate; and if they struggle to understand, we must try to help them. Once we have identified a given behaviour, we can ask them what other people might think when they behave in that way. Then we can ask them to suggest alternative ways to behave that would be more suitable, and how other people might react.

By using these strategies, we can help children with ADHD to prolong their reaction times and this helps them to manage their impulsivity, which is at the bottom of their aggressiveness and inappropriate emotional response to other people. The goal is to help them learn to stop in time, to reflect before reacting to what other people say and do, and to become aware of their own behaviour and of alternative ways of relating to other people to obtain more positive reactions from them.

Providing opportunities for positive social experiences in a setting where it is easier to be accepted by other children

As mentioned when speaking about ADHD and sports, it is helpful for these children to be involved in settings where they can demonstrate their abilities and feel more pleased with themselves, and thus have a more positive relationship with other people. We said before how school is a source of stress that can negatively influence these children's academic results, and it is a setting that demands a behavioural style at odds with the characteristics of ADHD. But in sporting and recreational settings, such as music groups, parish activities or scouts, these children can find their place more easily. In these settings they can be instantly gratified for what they do, feel their abilities are appreciated by their peers and the adults around them, be more relaxed in their social exchanges, and make friends. As we explain later in this chapter, when any child forms an opinion of one of their peers, it is hard to change. At school, this makes it difficult for children with ADHD to be appreciated, whereas in settings outside school (preferably chosen with these children's specific abilities in mind) it is easier for them to socialize and become integrated with their peers.

So, it is important to create opportunities for children with ADHD to socialize outside school. We can suggest they try other activities, and ask them what they would like to try. If the children voice no interest in taking part in any activities other than those organized at school, their parents can propose something in line with their aptitudes, maybe motivating them by rewarding them when they agree to have a go.

Use reinforcement every time children are even minimally successful in social settings

As explained already in previous chapters, one method that works very well with children and adolescents who have ADHD is reinforcement, which enables us to improve the chances of these children repeating the reinforced behaviour. Everything becomes more difficult in the case of social behaviour because the most critical situations develop at school. One way to proceed is to work together with the teachers, asking them to monitor the behaviour of children with ADHD, which will then be the object of reinforcements or consequences at home with their parents on the strength of the teacher's feedback. To give an idea, this means that if it has been agreed that a child must remember to raise their hand and wait their turn before speaking, whenever they succeed in doing so the teacher will attach a green sticker to their diary. If they answer impulsively and disregard this social rule, the teacher will attach a red sticker. After a child has been given three green stickers, their mother will buy them a pack of their favourite trading cards, but if they accumulate three red stickers they will not be allowed to use the PlayStation for two days. Here again, as explained in Chapters 4 and 5, it is important to have agreed beforehand with the child and put into writing what type of behaviour will earn them a reward.

For instance, they could be reinforced (earn a token) every time they lend something to a classmate, or pay a compliment to another child in class; and they could lose a token every time they are rude to a classmate. If we are unable to establish this type of cooperation with the teacher, and consequently cannot use a system of reinforcements and consequences at school, we will need to devise other ways to manage the child's social behaviour at home.

An accepting and welcoming attitude on the part of the teacher in class has proved very beneficial to the atmosphere at home as well. Clearly, we cannot generalize, and we must not forget that the way a child's classmates behave can vary and be hard to predict. Very often, especially when there are brothers and sisters involved, the situation at home can be very complicated and sometimes becomes unsustainable. Working on the social issues of children with ADHD at school can therefore be very important also in improving their behaviour at home.

A first approach, suitable for children from 9 to 10 years old, is to teach them to adopt an assertive communication modality. This involves the parents being the first to do so, as they are the child's fundamental role models. For further details on the assertive communication style, see Box 6.1.

Box 6.1 Assertiveness chart

There are various, more or less appropriate ways to ask other people for something you want. Asking for something appropriately involves communicating in an assertive manner. The term *assertive* may sound new: being assertive means communicating your opinions and preferences in a decisive, clear and honest manner. This means not bullying or being aggressive, but not being fearful or too concerned about other people's possible reactions either.

Decisive = when you ask for something, do so without hesitation or uncertainty;
Clear = accurately explain what you want;
Honest = speak your mind, but do not exploit a situation at someone else's expense.

Two inappropriate ways to make requests involve being aggressive or being passive. You communicate aggressively every time you let it show that you are angry, when you raise your voice, threaten, insult or sulk. You communicate passively whenever you seem hesitant, afraid, imploring or whining. Communicating your requests aggressively or passively makes both you and the people you are speaking to feel uncomfortable, whereas when you communicate assertively you feel more satisfied with yourself, and you have a better chance of getting what you want. Communication involves verbal expression, but also non-verbal aspects (gestures, posture, tone of voice, facial expression, eye contact), and what is not said can be just as important as what is said.

Assertive people are aware of their own and other people's rights. They are concerned about other people's feelings so their requests and critical comments tend to be voiced so as not to offend or worry others. They have a sense of give and take, and in conflictual situations they succeed in switching from a style of assertiveness to one of negotiation and cooperation.

Passive modality

People who adopt a passive approach tend to put other people's needs before their own. They often consider their needs less important than those of others, or they may not want to oppose others because they are afraid of being rejected or threatened. Even when they are dissatisfied with other people's choices they tend to accept them. Then, later on, they may suffer for having failed to follow through with their own demands and this can make them feel angry and resentful. Individuals who are very submissive also tend to lose other people's respect because they are considered incapable of standing up for themselves.

Aggressive modality

Aggressiveness takes shape in a tendency to promote your own ideas or wishes in an overpowering, bullying manner, stepping on other people's toes or hurting their feelings. Sometimes people with ADHD can be aggressive even when they believe that other people have the same rights as themselves, and this can be due to their excessive impulsivity. They may seem intimidating, but in the long run they tend to lose other people's respect. They also have difficulty making friends and keeping them because they are not good at expressing intimacy and affection.

Let us look at an example: Marta would like to be able to study in the early afternoon and then go out with her friends, but almost every afternoon Simona (who rarely goes out with other people) stops by for a chat. How can Marta explain to Simona that she would rather be left alone?

- Marta: "Okay, stay for a little while and I'll get back to my studies later."
- Marta: "Look, you should stop coming by when I'm not expecting you. I don't want to chat with you. Leave me in peace."
- Marta: "It's great to see you, but I need to study as soon as I get home from school so that I can be free later on. How about we choose Wednesdays as the day you come by for a chat?"

Think of the style corresponding to each type of answer, and whether you know someone who would be more likely to respond in one way rather than another. The first answer corresponds to a passive style, the second to an aggressive one and only the third is assertive: without showing any lack of respect for the other person, it still enables the speaker to say clearly what they want.

The core idea is that we need to express our emotions and ideas in a way that is respectful of ourselves and others. This communicational style is particularly useful when we need to manage troublesome situations. If it is used by parents, it serves as an example for their children. We suggest following the step-by-step outline below, always making eye contact with the person we are speaking to, keeping our tone of voice confident, using an appropriate volume and expressing ourselves simply and briefly.

1. Explain the problem objectively, without formulating judgements or personal opinions and without being sarcastic. For instance, we can imagine a situation where a mother tells her child: "When I ask you to switch off the PlayStation and come to the table for dinner, I would like you to do so straight away".
2. Explain how this problem makes you feel, and what emotions it arouses. For instance, "If you don't, it makes me feel sad and ignored, and then I get angry".
3. Suggest a solution to the problem that respects the other person, trying to mediate between what you want and what they want. For instance: "How about we agree to switch off the PlayStation at a quarter to eight, for instance, so that we're sure you're ready when it's time for dinner?". The child might oppose such a suggestion, but we can ask them to follow the same steps to try and find a compromise – always remembering to maintain eye contact and to use the same tone of voice and manner of speaking:

    •   "It doesn't seem to me that I don't come when you call me. Sometimes I don't hear you. Then I need a bit of time to finish the game, switch off and wash my hands"; or
    •   "I get cross because you seem to over-react, and also because on the occasions when I arrived before dinner was ready it looked like I was bothering you in the kitchen"; or
    •   "How about we decide a more or less set time for dinner, then I can be organized and so, by that time, I will have switched everything off, washed my hands and come to the table?".

Another aspect to bear in mind is the need to avoid drawing comparisons between children with ADHD and their siblings or other children. This seems obvious enough, but sometimes – without wishing to do so, or with the best intentions of motivating a child – a parent may say: "Look at how well behaved that child is, sitting nicely at the table … not like you" (the last three words might be spoken aloud or only implicit). Or, on hearing that their child got a pass in a subject in which they were struggling, the parent might say: "Ah, that's great, but how did your friend so-and-so get on?", ... and the friend usually got higher marks. Even within the family, a parent could unwittingly say: "Your room's a disaster! Look at how good your sister is at keeping everything tidy!", or "It's unbeliev-able. I never had so much trouble getting your brother to do his homework!". Comments of this kind can feel like a punch in the stomach, weighing heavily on a child's mood. As we wrote earlier, children with ADHD are often not really aware of their problems. What they do notice is that very often, try as they might, they struggle to do what they are asked, and other people get impatient with them even when they think they have behaved nicely. Instead of stimulating them to do better, comments like those mentioned above tend to demoralize them, partly because they fail to take the child's ADHD into account. Instead, they remind these youngsters – yet again – that they are unable to do what is expected of them, whereas other chil-dren, their classmates and siblings, manage just fine. So, it is more useful to explain to these children what they can do to improve their behaviour, and help them with their issues. It is important to ensure they understand that every one of us has strengths and weaknesses, and if we acknowledge them, we can work on the weaknesses and find the right way to make the best of our abilities.

Finally, based also on everything we have said so far, it is certainly essential to support children with ADHD, to have faith in them and to avoid making them feel guilty about their difficulties. Instead, we can help them to think over certain situations after the event and, if necessary, try and work out what went wrong and how they could have managed the situ-ation better; and we can reinforce and gratify them whenever they have got things right. The core idea is that every child should be in the best position to express the best of their abil-ities, and the price they pay for their difficulties should be kept to a minimum. This is a constant challenge when dealing with children who have ADHD, but we can gain enormous satisfac-tion when we succeed.

The school's role in accepting and managing the social difficulties associated with ADHD

As we have already seen, school is a very important place for every child because it is where they learn how to relate to others (children and adults), as well as acquiring academic skills. Relations with classmates provide the first training ground outside the family where children learn to cooperate, negotiate and solve conflicts. It is fundamentally important that we all learn these skills to ensure our effective social functioning for the rest of our lives in every situation we may encounter (Hoza, 2007).

Treatments such as psychoactive drugs and behavioural management techniques are useful for improving the symptoms of ADHD, but cannot have any direct effect on the classroom setting. In fact, they have proved to have little effect on the social functioning of pupils with ADHD. This is partly because these children have a limited capacity for transferring skills learned in one setting to other situations, and partly because they come up against the huge difficulty of making their classmates change their opinion of them (Abikoff et al., 2004; Mrug, Hoza, & Gerdes, 2001).

Questionnaires can be administered to assess children's relations with their classmates. Each pupil answers questions about which of their classmates they prefer to have sitting next to them, or on their teams, or to spend time with during break (Capodieci, Rivetti, & Cornoldi, 2019; Rivetti & Capodieci, 2017). It has been demonstrated that the same sort of behaviour on the part of a given child is interpreted differently by their classmates depending on the child's popularity. In other words, their peers are prepared to grant the benefit of the doubt about certain dubious behaviour to children they already like, whereas a child who is not very popular may be judged negatively if they behave in the same way. As a result, even when the behaviour of children with ADHD improves, it seems unlikely that their classmates will change their opinion of them. That is why the role of parents and teachers is so important in shaping the other children's opinions, and succeeding in influencing them positively, especially while these children are still in primary school (Mikami, Griggs, Reuland, & Gregory, 2012).

In fact, research has shown that teachers who personally appreciate and accept children with behavioural problems make it easier for the other children in the class to tolerate such children's unusual behaviour. Vice versa, if teachers criticize their behaviour or show their frustration with these children, they make them more liable to be rejected by their peers (McAuliffe, Hubbard, & Romano, 2009). This has to do with the so-called "Pygmalion effect" (see Box 6.2); if a teacher believes that a given child is less talented than the others they will treat them differently, even without being aware of it. The child accepts this judgement and the message transmitted by this

---

Box 6.2 The Pygmalion effect

The *Pygmalion effect*, or *self-fulfilling prophecy*, is a form of psychological suggestion such that people tend to conform to other people's idea of them. Some researchers administered intelligence tests to a group of primary school pupils, then randomly extracted some of these children and led both the children and their teachers to believe that they were of above-average intelligence. A year later, these children's academic performance had improved. The teachers had positively influenced them with their attitude, unaware of the fact that it had only been a suggestion (Rosenthal, 2002). This goes to show how important it is for adults serving as a reference to send a clear message regarding a child's characteristics, and for them to reinforce any positive behaviour and emphasize the child's strengths and skills instead of labelling them for their misbehaviour or inappropriate attitude.

---

reference figure, and will behave according to the teacher's expectations. This has a cascading effect and the child will gradually become what the teacher had imagined. This goes to show why the classroom should be seen as one of the main places for intervention in the social problems of children with ADHD since it is the main stage for their social interactions.

At this point it is clear that educational practices can have a key impact on these aspects of life in class. To give an example, watching an experimentally manipulated video showing a teacher giving positive feedback to an unpopular classmate induced the other children to change their perception of this child (White & Eiledh McGarry, 2000). As various researchers have suggested, training teachers to cope with behavioural problems and make the group of peers more inclusive can have a positive effect on children with ADHD, and on children with special educational needs in general (Mikami, Reuland, Griggs, Jia, & Suldo, 2013). A durable change in teachers' attitudes can also help children with ADHD to avoid being rejected by their peers in subsequent classes.

Two of the most effective strategies for improving inclusion, that can be used both in class and in afternoon study settings, are peer tutoring and cooperative learning.

Peer tutoring. Numerous formulas have been used to provide a detailed definition of this activity, one of which describes it as an approach where one child teaches another child something on a subject on which the former is more expert than the latter (Damon & Phelps, 1989). It can involve activities for pairs of children of the same age (same-age peer tutoring) or different ages (cross-age peer tutoring), without going into the question of any difference in expertise existing between the two children involved. More recently, the term has been defined as the acquisition of knowledge and skills through active help and support, provided by people from a similar social group (Topping, 2005).

Children taking part in peer tutoring gain in terms of their self-perception as learners and there are changes in their social functioning too: children and adolescents learn to adopt a more desirable behaviour, to share and to listen to people who think differently (Madrid, Canas, & Ortega-Medina, 2007). Finally, peer tutoring promotes a greater acceptance of classmates with various disorders, including ADHD, and those of different socio-cultural origins. The opportunity to cooperate with another person of the same age enables children to understand how even classmates who seem very different actually have many more aspects in common than they might have expected (Ginsburg-Block, Rohrbeck, & Fantuzzo, 2006).

In peer tutoring, teachers share a part of their responsibility for teaching with their pupils, turning them into facilitators of their classmates' learning. This also gives teachers the chance to focus on providing feedback for each and every pupil, something difficult to achieve during their activities conducted with the class as a whole (Stenhoff & Lignugaris/Kraft, 2007). Peer tutoring thus seems to be a genuinely valid, inclusive method that helps children with ADHD, and can be beneficial to every other member of the class as well.

Cooperative learning. Among the various other educational practices used in class, cooperative learning seems to be one of those with the most positive implications for children with ADHD. Cooperative learning involves students working in small groups organized in such a way as to enable them to achieve shared goals. It is amply recognized as a teaching strategy that promotes learning and socialization among students of all ages and in various academic disciplines. It has been used successfully to improve students' academic results and their willingness to work cooperatively and productively with other students who may have different needs and levels of learning, and it facilitates group relations with children of different backgrounds. Cooperative learning can enable:

- better interpersonal relations between the students;
- a greater respect for, and acknowledgement of each other as competent individuals;
- a greater awareness of other people's points of view and different perspectives;
- an empowerment of creative thinking, because it facilitates communication and the sharing of lots of ideas.

The students actively involved learn to reason together on problems and to interact routinely with one another under the teacher's guidance. This enables them to understand their mutual differences and learn how to solve social problems that may develop when they work together (Felder & Brent, 2007; Slavin, 2011).

There are several important aspects to consider when organizing lessons to be conducted according to the cooperative learning method (Johnson, Johnson, & Smith, 2007).

Positive interdependence. This is when participants see that they can achieve their own goals if and only if the other participants in the group achieve their goals too, so it is only the sum of all their efforts that produces the shared results.

Individual and group responsibility. This is when every child's performance is monitored and feedback on the results is given both to the individuals and to the group. Every group member is held responsible for the others, and thus contributes to the success of the group of a whole.

Promotional face-to-face interaction. To be mutually encouraging, members of the group help and support each other, sharing the necessary resources (information and materials), offering each other feedback, challenging each other's conclusions and motives, so they will be better prepared when they have to do these things outside the group in future.

Using social skills. Some abilities, such as decision-making, managing communications and solving conflicts, must be taught with the same attention as academic skills. To coordinate their efforts to achieve their shared goals, students must:

- get to know and trust each other;
- communicate accurately and unambiguously;
- accept and support each other;
- solve conflicts constructively.

When the students learn these social skills (which are essential to good-quality cooperation) and they are motivated to use them, then cooperative learning groups become highly productive. The more the students are socially capable, and the teachers and parents pay attention and reward their use of their social skills, the better the results that we can expect from cooperative learning groups.

Although cooperative learning has been accepted as an important teaching strategy, the difficulties inherent in adopting this approach can explain the tendency of educators to exclude hyperactive or inattentive students from such group experiences. A recent study on this topic investigated the effects of cooperative learning intervention on relations between classmates in some primary school classes where there were also children with a diagnosis or symptoms of ADHD (Capodieci et al., 2019). The cooperative learning activities forming the object of the study were introduced gradually, enabling the children to first learn certain basic social skills, practice communicating with others and solving interpersonal problems, and then work together towards shared academic goals. The study findings showed a specific improvement in the children with symptoms of ADHD who took part in the cooperative learning sessions. In particular, after the period of cooperative learning, there was an increase in the number of classmates who wanted to play with these children or chose them as team mates. There was also a trend towards an improvement in the number of peers who wanted a child with symptoms of ADHD sitting next to them. A crucial feature of this particular study lies in that the children with symptoms of ADHD worked together with the other children in the class: this probably made it easier for them to get to know each other, and promoted a mutual exchange of needs and help (e.g. Abikoff et al., 2004; Chew, Jensen, & Rosén, 2009; Mikami et al., 2013).

This brings us to the question that families often ask, about whether it is useful or even necessary to share their child's diagnosis of ADHD with the school and their friends, and how much the child may risk being labelled and treated differently as a consequence. The answer depends on the type of teachers and friends involved, and whether or not the child has other comorbid disorders. If we are dealing with a teacher who has received appropriate training and is attentive to the needs of individual children, they will have been trying to facilitate such students' learning even without being informed of their diagnosis. In such cases, it is useful to involve them, notify them of the diagnosis and provide details of the child's symptoms and any comorbidities. The diagnosis can also be shared with the class at the family's explicit request and, in this case, it would be advisable for the school to promote a campaign of awareness about inclusion and diversity, paying attention to the particular features of each and every student, and their need for help and mutual support. Such schemes make school life more straightforward and pleasant for everybody concerned, students and teachers. In recent years, there have been increasingly numerous projects in schools focusing on psychological issues. We judge it important for these initiatives to include laboratories to explain to students that all sorts of diversity, not only in matters of origin, religion and language (which may be difficult to deal with, but are certainly easier for children to understand), but also in different individuals' manner of learning, academic needs and personal traits, which may necessitate particular teaching methods.

It often happens that children or adolescents with ADHD are afraid of using the special support services and tools to which they are entitled because they worry about being judged as "different" by their classmates (Sironi, Vicenza, Cataldi, Frinco, Frinco, & Sini, 2019). I remember when I asked one 14-year-old why he wanted nobody to know about his diagnosis of ADHD at his new school, where he had started a few months earlier with very poor results, he said:

> Yeah, I did much better at school last year, but the only friends I had were the other two certified children in the class, one disabled and one with an autistic spectrum disorder. I'd rather do badly at school but be able to have lots of friends and ordinary relations with all my classmates, without them judging me.

Such situations are unfortunately common and, when parents ask what they can do to improve matters, it is not easy to give them an answer. But there is one thing that any adult whose profession or life choices (parents, sports trainers, educators) mean they deal with children should bear in mind: the important message to convey is that everyone has their own peculiarities. Many children at school do not have particular academic difficulties, but may be unable to take up the sport they would like because they lack good coordination. Others do not play a musical instrument because they have no sense of rhythm. Others may be able to practice any kind of sport, or play any kind of musical instrument, but need specific teaching methods in class and special learning tools to help them work as successfully as their classmates, stay concentrated and not behave impulsively. Then there are those who may have difficulty both in sports and academically, but who are very popular because they have a special sensitivity: they understand their friends' state of mind and succeed in being a comfort to others. One of the important things for parents and teachers to do is to make children aware of the value of diversity right from a very early age. As they grow up, children need to be loved, but they also need to know they are okay just as they are. If they learn and experience this feeling for themselves, they will also know how to accept others for what they are, in every aspect.

Communication of the diagnosis

"So, if my child asks me what they can or should tell friends and classmates about their diagnosis, and how they should go about it, what should I say?" Clearly, there is more to this issue than a right and a wrong answer. Parents need to discuss this together with their child, trying to understand what is best on the basis of the child's characteristics and those of their friends and classmates.

First of all, it is important to understand why the child feels the need to share their problem with others. There may be several reasons. For instance: because they sometimes feel different or feel that others do not understand them; or out of a sense of loyalty because the teachers use different strategies with them and this can be a cause of embarrassment, or they worry their classmates will notice, or find out from someone else. In the former case, if the child thinks it best to tell a couple of friends they trust about their diagnosis, and they expect them to understand, this could make them feel better about themselves. In that case, we can help them to find the right words to explain their particular characteristics as simply as possible, and why they sometimes seem to be forgetful, unreliable, irritating and so on. In the latter case, it is important for the child not to feel obliged to explain themselves. It would be better for the school to improve the students' awareness of the importance of acknowledging and respecting diversity, and the value intrinsic in every individual that others must know how to appreciate. But if the child is keen to tell their classmates about their diagnosis of ADHD, it is advisable to schedule this appropriately. It is important for this to be done under the teacher's supervision and to be properly organized to avoid the risk of the child being taunted or misunderstood. It can also be helpful to bring examples or show films that help the others understand the issue, or use games involving social skills that facilitate the inclusion of children who have had the courage to talk to the class about their disorder.

ADHD and social media

Parents very often see "social media" as a diabolical waste of time for their children with ADHD because it tends to keep them at home, shut in their own rooms to chat and look at what other people are doing, occupying their time in a way that almost always seems pointless. While this can be true if social media is misused, it is also true that it can serve as a different way to enter into contact with other people. It can provide access to communities of young people with ADHD where everyone can feel accepted and share their experiences, which are often not understood by those around them in the real world (be they parents, friends, family members or teachers). These websites can also be a place and an opportunity for joking about why these youngsters are always being rebuked, or for gaining a better understanding of why they behave the way they do. This gives them a greater awareness of the disorder without making them feel embarrassed. A few examples of such groups on Instagram are: *adhdworldwide, adhdpeople, adhdmems*. In all the social networks, there are also the official groups of associations like the ADHD Foundation.

Adhdpeople was created by a 16-year-old Swedish girl with ADHD who wants people with this diagnosis to feel they are not alone. *Adhdworldwide* was developed by a woman with ADHD who tries to make other people understand what she is like as a person on her good days and on the days when her ADHD makes everything more difficult. Among the comments about ADHD in their profiles we read, for instance:

> "You said ADHD isn't real and I can even say being normal isn't real."
> "I have more thoughts before breakfast than probably you have all day."
> "If a child can't learn the way you teach, maybe you should teach the way he learns."
> "Try to pay more attention to the intention."

There are also various comments on the occasions when people with ADHD met with psychological difficulties and had problems managing their daily lives. Questions are posed to drive the debate, such as: How do you get people without the disorder to understand what it is like to have ADHD? What are the things that most bother you about the disorder? Are there any aspects of ADHD that you accept and appreciate?

Talking about their problems and having an opportunity to do so in a setting where they feel safer and better understood, and discussing their ideas, their fears and especially what they see as their potential strengths can be very helpful for young people with ADHD. On the other hand, as in everything else, even in these situations some of them still risk feeling misunderstood. That is why, as already mentioned in Chapter 5, it is important for these young people to have an adult they can refer to (a family member, an educator in a parish group or sports trainer, a professional such as a psychologist or psychiatrist), who can help them to make good use of these tools.

References

Abikoff, H., Hechtman, L., Klein, R. G., Weiss, G., Fleiss, K., Etcovitch, J. O. Y., ... Pollack, S. (2004). Symptomatic improvement in children with ADHD treated with long-term methylphenidate and multimodal psychosocial treatment. *Journal of the American Academy of Child & Adolescent Psychiatry, 43*(7), 802–811.

Bagwell, C. L., Molina, B. S., Pelham, W. E., Jr, & Hoza, B. (2001). Attention-deficit hyperactivity disorder and problems in peer relations:

Predictions from childhood to adolescence. *Journal of the American Academy of Child & Adolescent Psychiatry*, *40*(11), 1285–1292.

Capodieci, A., Rivetti, T., & Cornoldi, C. (2019). A cooperative learning classroom intervention for increasing peer's acceptance of children with ADHD. *Journal of Attention Disorders*, *23*(3), 282–292.

Chew, B. L., Jensen, S. A., & Rosén, L. A. (2009). College students' attitudes toward their ADHD peers. *Journal of Attention Disorders*, *13*(3), 271–276.

Damon, W., & Phelps, E. (1989). Critical distinctions among three approaches to peer education. *International Journal of Educational Research*, *13*(1), 9–19.

Dendy, C. A. Z. (2011). *Teaching teens with ADD, ADHD & executive function deficits: A quick reference guide for teachers and parents*. Bethesda, MD: Woodbine House.

Felder, R. M., & Brent, R. (2007). *Cooperative learning*. Washington, DC: ACS Publication.

Ginsburg-Block, M. D., Rohrbeck, C. A., & Fantuzzo, J. W. (2006). A meta-analytic review of social, self-concept, and behavioral outcomes of peer-assisted learning. *Journal of Educational Psychology*, *98*(4), 732–749.

Greene, R. W., Biederman, J., Faraone, S. V., Sienna, M., & Garcia-Jetton, J. (1997). Adolescent outcome of boys with attention-deficit/hyperactivity disorder and social disability: Results from a 4-year longitudinal follow-up study. *Journal of Consulting and Clinical Psychology*, *65*(5), 758–767.

Hoza, B. (2007). Peer functioning in children with ADHD. *Journal of Pediatric Psychology*, *32*(6), 655–663.

Johnson, D. W., Johnson, R. T., & Smith, K. (2007). The state of cooperative learning in postsecondary and professional settings. *Educational Psychology Review*, *19*(1), 15–29.

Madrid, L. D., Canas, M., & Ortega-Medina, M. (2007). Effects of team competition versus team cooperation in classwide peer tutoring. *The Journal of Educational Research*, *100*(3), 155–160.

McAuliffe, M. D., Hubbard, J. A., & Romano, L. J. (2009). The role of teacher cognition and behavior in children's peer relations. *Journal of Abnormal Child Psychology*, *37*(5), 665–677.

Mikami, A. Y., Griggs, M. S., Reuland, M. M., & Gregory, A. (2012). Teacher practices as predictors of children's classroom social preference. *Journal of School Psychology*, *50*(1), 95–111.

Mikami, A. Y., & Hinshaw, S. P. (2006). Resilient adolescent adjustment among girls: Buffers of childhood peer rejection and attention-deficit/hyperactivity disorder. *Journal of Abnormal Child Psychology*, *34*(6), 823–837.

Mikami, A. Y., Reuland, M. M., Griggs, M. S., Jia, M., & Suldo, S. (2013). Collateral effects of a peer relationship intervention for children with attention deficit hyperactivity disorder on typically developing classmates. *School Psychology Review*, 42(4), 458–476.

Mrug, S., Hoza, B., & Gerdes, A. C. (2001). Children with attention-deficit/hyperactivity disorder: Peer relationships and peer-oriented interventions. In D. W. Nangle & C. A. Erdley (Eds.), *New directions for child and adolescent development. The role of friendship in psychological adjustment, No. 91*. San Francisco: Jossey-Bass.

Rivetti, T., & Capodieci, A. (2017). Apprendimento cooperativo personalizzato. Attività per la classe con bambini con ADHD o problemi di comportamento [Personalized cooperative learning. Class activities with children with ADHD or behaviour problems]. Trento, Italy: Erickson.

Rosenthal, R. (2002). The Pygmalion effect and its mediating mechanisms. In *Improving academic achievement* (pp. 25–36). Cambridge, MA: Academic Press.

Sironi, E. M., Vicenza, P., Cataldi, N., Frinco, L., Frinco, M., & Sini, B. (2019). Reazioni alla diagnosi di DSA e componenti emotive e cognitive che influiscono sull'uso degli strumenti compensativi e delle misure dispensative. L'opinione di 100 studenti con DSA. [Reactions to the diagnosis of DSA and emotional and cognitive components that influence the use of compensatory tools and dispensative measures. The opinion of 100 students with DSA]. *Psicologia Clinica dello Sviluppo, XXIII*, 1, 97–115.

Slavin, R. E. (2011). Cooperative learning. *Learning and Cognition in Education Elsevier Academic Press, Boston*, 160–166.

Stenhoff, D. M., & Lignugaris/Kraft, B. (2007). A review of the effects of peer tutoring on students with mild disabilities in secondary settings. *Exceptional Children*, 74(1), 8–30.

Topping, K. J. (2005). Trends in peer learning. *Educational psychology*, 25(6), 631–645.

White, R. J., & Eiledh McGarry, J. (2000). Cognitive behavioural computer therapy for the anxiety disorders: A pilot study. *Journal of Mental Health*, 9(5), 505–516.

Chapter 7

Cultural differences and sensitivities

Introduction

Research has shown that ADHD is being diagnosed and treated in more and more countries worldwide. Epidemiological data also indicate that its treatment with psychoactive drugs is constantly on the rise. Until the early 1990s, few published studies on the diagnosis and treatment of ADHD came from outside the United States, giving the impression that it was a disorder related to the North American way of life. Recent international research has shown that this impression was wrong.

In this chapter, we take a look at aspects relating to the diagnosis and treatment of ADHD in various countries in the Americas, Europe, Asia and Africa. We begin with the United States because it is where this disorder first came to light. Then we move on to the countries most influenced by American culture, Canada and Australia, before shifting the focus to Europe. There, we begin with the English-speaking countries, the United Kingdom and Ireland, then we examine the situation in Germany, Italy and France. Leaving Europe behind, we consider some countries in Latin America, Argentina, Brazil and Chile, before moving on to Asia to look at Japan and Taiwan, and then to Africa, where we consider Ghana.

But first we need to say a few words on the different usage of the diagnostic manuals (the DSM-5 and the ICD-10) in the various countries we discuss. Americans tend to rely exclusively on the DSM-5 (APA, 2013), while Europeans also refer to the ICD-10 (WHO, 2010). European public health services usually adopt the ICD-10, while researchers and professionals in private practice prefer the DSM-5. The wording used by the ICD-10 is *hyperkinetic conduct disorder* and a diagnosis of this condition requires *all* the typical symptoms of ADHD (inattention, hyperactivity and impulsivity). On the other hand, any one of these symptoms suffices for a diagnosis of ADHD according to the DSM-5. As we can easily imagine, this means a different prevalence of the disorder depending on which manual is taken for reference.

Below we review the international scene to see which aspects of ADHD are shared and contribute to the "global" picture of the disorder. Then, looking more closely, we identify certain diagnostic, therapeutic and legislative criteria, and issues relating to the stigma associated with the disorder, that are characteristic of a given country, adding "local" facets to the international concept of ADHD.

ADHD in the United States

The United States has always been one of the countries with the highest incidence of ADHD in terms of the number of cases being diagnosed and treated. There are currently 8.8% of school-aged children in the United States with a diagnosis of ADHD, and 69% of them are given pharmacological treatment (Conrad & Bergey, 2014; Visser et al., 2014). The disorder's official recognition in the DSM and the latest editions' emphasis on its persistence throughout a person's life have revealed the need for individuals with ADHD to be supported because their condition can influence their academic/occupational performance and social adjustment.

That is why ADHD was included among the disabilities covered by the Individuals with Disabilities Act (IDEA) in 1991. This legislation is designed to ensure that public funding is available so that children and adolescents with disabilities can have an adequate education. Cases of ADHD can be included in one of three categories depending on any comorbidities and a given child's particular difficulties, i.e. specific learning disorders, major emotional disorders or other medical problems. Children with ADHD who fit into one of these categories have access to an individualized education and special public health services (Reid, Maag, & Vasa, 1993). When they grow up, adults with ADHD can likewise refer to the Americans with Disabilities Act (ADA), which protects them on a social and occupational level (Conrad & Potter, 2000). With the IDEA and the ADA, a diagnosis of ADHD fits into a broader category of disabilities for which a greater degree of support is assured in all aspects of an individual's life.

A fundamental factor in the picture of ADHD in the United States concerns the increasing use of treatment with psychoactive drugs. This was one of the issues that brought ADHD to the attention of the general public in the 1970s and it is still a debated topic. The first drug used in this setting was Ritalin (methylphenidate), which was originally indicated not for hyperactivity, but for depression, lethargy and chronic fatigue. It was prescribed "off-label" in paediatric psychiatry wards (Singh, 2006). After a number of case studies, it became the treatment of choice for ADHD up until the 1990s, when other drugs started to emerge on the market (Adderall, Concerta, Vyvanse).

The number of children treated pharmacologically in the United States is constantly increasing. The annual rate of growth in the use of psychoactive drugs, for example, is 3.4% (Zuvekas & Vitiello, 2012). Pharmaceutical companies invest a great deal of money in promoting this type of treatment, one of the consequences of which is a lesser investment in terms of services, and they often support organizations and associations concerned with ADHD. There is ongoing debate on the role that these companies should or should not have in various settings (Timimi, 2008).

Some interesting information that emerges from North American data concerns the relationship between the diagnosis of ADHD and factors including gender, ethnicity and family characteristics such as income, the mother's level of education, the language spoken, the geographical area of residence and the type of healthcare insurance. There is evidence of an over-diagnosis of ADHD in white children by comparison with ethnic minorities (Morgan, Staff, Hillemeier, Farkas, & Maczuga, 2013), in children who speak English as their first language as opposed to other languages and in those belonging to families who have healthcare insurance as opposed to those who do not (Visser et al., 2014). There is a larger proportion of children with ADHD in single-parent families than among children living with both parents (Bloom, Jones, & Freeman, 2013). As for geographical region, there is a higher likelihood of being diagnosed with ADHD in the south of the United States than in the east: the percentages range from 4% to 5% in some states (Nevada, New Jersey) to 14–15% in others (Arkansas, Kentucky). Boys are still diagnosed more often than girls, even though the difference in the proportion of males and females with the disorder has virtually disappeared according to the latest version of the diagnostic manual (NSCH, 2016).

New issues regarding ADHD in the United States

Among the topics most recently discussed, one that has aroused interest concerns the expansion in recent years of a "black market" for psychoactive drugs among students who have not been diagnosed with ADHD. They purchase these drugs without a prescription to improve their concentration, in the hope of enhancing their cognitive and academic performance (McCabe, 2008; Singh, Filipe, Bard, Bergey, & Baker, 2013; see also the section below on Germany).

Another delicate topic concerns the likelihood of the number of diagnoses continuing to rise. The publication of the latest issue of the DSM-5 has coincided with a trend in this direction because fewer symptoms are required (five instead of six) to establish the diagnosis in adolescents and adults, and the age by which symptoms must become apparent has been extended to 12 years old instead of seven. The new guidelines of the American Academy of Paediatrics (AAP, 2011) also envisage the possibility of diagnosing and treating ADHD in preschool-aged children.

More and more efforts are being made to promote psycho-social interventions specifically for managing the symptoms of ADHD, to be provided in association with pharmacological and/or psychological treatments. Such interventions have become widespread particularly in the last 10–15 years. They are conducted by coaches, individuals who have ADHD themselves or members of families that have children with the disorder. These interventions have emerged to respond to the dissatisfaction of people with ADHD, who complain of feeling misunderstood by healthcare professionals. Coaches help these people to gain a better understanding of their diagnosis and difficulties, and suggest strategies for managing them more effectively. They also focus strongly on these people's strengths, teaching them how to make the best of their qualities (Bergey, 2015).

Finally, ADHD has spread from being a North American problem to being a worldwide phenomenon over the last 20 years. This has happened for various reasons, including: a greater awareness of the disorder, partly thanks to information and checklists available on the Internet; promotion schemes run by pharmaceutical companies; and a growth in the number of associations supporting people with ADHD and improving the public's understanding of the condition (Bergey, Filipe, Conrad, & Singh, 2018).

Canada

Initially, Canada always tended to follow in the footsteps of the United States concerning the diagnosis and treatment of ADHD, as for other mental health issues. This approach was facilitated by the diffusion of the American media, the use of American websites by healthcare professionals and of US blogs by families of children with ADHD, and, more generally, the presence of American culture in countless Canadian information settings. It is only more recently that professionals and support groups have made some effort to detach themselves from the American model in favour of a new, specifically Canadian approach (Malacrida & Semach, 2018).

The country's criticism of the US model mainly concerns its massive use of psychoactive drugs, even for small children. According to the National Longitudinal Study Survey of Children and Youth, among school-aged children and pre-schoolers the prevalence of the diagnosis of ADHD in Canada is 3.7% for boys and 1.5% for girls (Charach, Lin, & To, 2010).

There were no proper guidelines on how to establish a diagnosis of ADHD in Canada until 2006. The assessment protocols varied, depending on who the parents consulted and where. Some only conducted interviews with parents or administered them questionnaires, others also investigated the reported symptoms by contacting teachers and educators, and some simply tested the drug on the child to see whether it had any effect (Malacrida, 2004). In 2006, a national not-for-profit group of professionals – the Canadian ADHD Research Alliance (CADDRA) – published its first guidelines in the hope of having them adopted as standard practice throughout the country (CADDRA, 2011). The group considered the guidelines adopted in the United States and United Kingdom, noting their contradictory approaches: the former recommends pharmacological treatment as the first choice and other treatments as a second option; the latter suggests that pharmacological treatments are only warranted in severe cases. The group of Canadian specialists came up with guidelines that come somewhere in between the previous two proposals. Their holistic model included psycho-education for patients and their families, behavioural strategies, psychotherapy and tools to aid learning at school and productivity in the workplace, plus pharmacological treatment as a way to facilitate the other measures. The idea of using medication to support other interventions was optimistic, however, judging from the actual situation of treatments for ADHD in Canada.

It is worth adding that the costs of medical and psychiatric care for ADHD are covered by the insurance schemes, while psychotherapies are not. As a consequence, poorer people are often just given pharmacological treatment, while those who can afford them also benefit from other types of intervention. Unfortunately, there is also still little communication between the parties involved in managing children with ADHD. Some children are simply given pharmacological therapy, while there is no cooperation between parents, teachers and specialists to help them improve as a whole. In the long run, this can also lead to a poor compliance with the pharmacological therapy (Edmunds & Martsch-Litt, 2008).

Australia

Like Canada, Australia has also used North American culture for reference ever since the 1950s, particularly on matters of health and medicine. This has translated into a preference for the pharmacological treatment of ADHD since the 1970s.

The estimated prevalence of ADHD in Australia is between 6% and 9% of the paediatric population (Al-Yagon et al., 2013). The prescription of psychoactive drugs increased enormously through the 1990s and into the early 2000s. The marked growth in the cases of ADHD diagnosed and treated pharmacologically ultimately captured the attention of general public and professionals alike. This led in 1997 to the issue of the first Australian guidelines for assessing and managing ADHD, published by the Australian National Health and Medical Research Council (NHMRC, 1997). These guidelines take the DSM-IV for reference and adopt a strictly medical approach. In fact, despite recommending a treatment based on a multimodal approach, the only practical indications they provide concern the pharmacological treatment of ADHD. This has led to an increase both in the number of cases diagnosed and in the prescription of psychoactive drugs to treat them, prompting professionals and associations to voice their concern about this situation. To make matters worse, basic medical insurance for Australian citizens covers the costs of professionals such as paediatricians and psychiatrists, but not of other specialists, thus making pharmacological treatment more economical and accessible than a multimodal approach. An important aspect to mention is that Australian students with disabilities are included in regular classes at school (according to an inclusive education approach), where they have access to benefits and support. The problem is that ADHD is not included among the six categories of disability for which children are entitled to help, which is only available for children with physical, visual or hearing disabilities, moderate or severe cognitive disabilities, autistic spectrum disorders, or mental health problems. That is why, in addition to a diagnosis of ADHD, many children are also diagnosed with an autistic spectrum disorder; or else an initial diagnosis of ADHD or oppositional defiant disorder, or conduct disorder, is replaced with a diagnosis of autism.

Attempts were recently made on several occasions to update Australia's initial guidelines, but it was twice necessary to backtrack because of criticism over the excessive direct or indirect influence of the pharmaceutical companies on the decision-making process. Finally, in 2011, the NHMRC drafted its "Clinical practice points for consultation" based – according to their critics – on a convenient compromise between pro-medical and anti-pharmaceutical opinions rather than on a consensus on scientific evidence, and produced by a committee that included both supporters and sceptics regarding the use of medication for ADHD. These practical recommendations are rather brief, and concentrate mainly on interventions to be used by psychiatrists and neuropsychologists (NHMRC, 2012). Little reference is made to the provision of support at school, or any other type of help, and there is nothing about socio-cultural influences on the behaviour of children with ADHD or how the disorder should be interpreted. These questions might be dealt with more appropriately in a series of guidelines that were due to be published in 2014, but for now nothing is known about whether they have actually been prepared or published. At the time of writing, Australia therefore still has no formal guidelines on the management of ADHD (Prosser & Graham, 2018).

United Kingdom

In the United Kingdom, the study of ADHD can be conceptualized as revolving around a set of genetic and brain markers, complex cognitive endophenotypes and research. This approach has had the effect of limiting the general public's acceptance and understanding of the diagnosis and treatment of ADHD. It is easy to imagine that this has a negative fallout on the families and children needing to engage in the process for assessing and treating the disorder. It also does nothing to help contain the related stigma. On the other hand, it means that the use of pharmacological treatments for ADHD is not as widespread as in other countries (Singh, 2018).

Clinical practice in the country is regulated by the National Institute for Clinical and Care Excellence (NICE), which systematically reviews the scientific evidence on diagnostic and treatment practices and the best practice guidelines. Based on a balance of costs, benefits and evidence, NICE indicates which treatments are to be covered by the National Health Service (NHS).

NICE also refers to the use of both the diagnostic manuals, the DSM and the ICD-10, and specifies the need to report the criteria of the manual adopted in guidelines for clinicians. The two manuals are associated with a different prevalence of ADHD in the population. In 2013, NICE estimated that between 3% and 9% of children have the disorder according to the DSM-IV, whereas only 1–2% of children would meet the criteria of the ICD-10. Since the NHS adopts the ICD-10, we can assume that only moderate-to-severe cases of ADHD are diagnosed in the United Kingdom. A recent systematic analysis calculated that between 1.9% and 5% of children in the United Kingdom meet the criteria for ADHD (Murphy, McCarthy, Baer, Zima, & Jellinek, 2014).

According to the NICE guidelines, pharmacological treatment should only be recommended as the first choice for the most severe cases. Judging from the available data on the pharmacological treatments administered, compliance with these recommendations seems to be fairly consistent: between 0.02% and 3% of children and adolescents between 3 and 18 years old take medication for ADHD, making the United Kingdom's one of the lowest prevalence rates in the world.

In the case of mild-to-moderate ADHD, the first choice of treatment is parent training (NICE) and psychotherapy for the child (ADHD Quality Standard, NICE, 2013).

As concerns education, schooling is compulsory up to 16 years old and the majority of children attend state schools or officially recognized denominational schools. Only 4% of children in the United Kingdom go to fee-paying private schools. Children with ADHD are not acknowledged as having a disability and are consequently not automatically selected for special education services. Parents can ask for their child to be acknowledged as having special educational needs in two different ways: through special education services provided by schools or using a national legal instrument called the "Education, health and care plan". Neither route is easy to travel. In the former case, schools do not always have sufficient resources to provide special education services for all the children needing them. In the latter, it is difficult for children with a diagnosis of ADHD to be granted this type of public intervention. Given these issues, the relationship and cooperation between schools and families becomes particularly important. This cooperation is often sadly lacking, however, especially in more socio-economically disadvantaged family situations and areas (Blum, 2015), although it has been shown to improve the likelihood of children with ADHD changing their behaviour, and thus reducing the risk of being accused of misbehaving or being lazy.

The best-known support organization for ADHD, and the first to be established in the United Kingdom, is called the Attention Deficit Disorder Information and Support Service. Its primary role is to serve as an information centre, but it has recently begun to offer training for professionals and educators.

Another organization established in recent years, the ADHD Foundation, works to promote inclusion, education and employment opportunities for people with the disorder. In 2009, a group of mental health professionals created the UK Adult ADHD Network.

Ireland

Now let us take a look at the United Kingdom's nearest neighbour and say a few words on the situation regarding ADHD in Ireland. An important contribution to its acceptance as a neuropsychological disorder came from the organizations providing support for ADHD sufferers. This involved a battle that intensified, and was won, between the end of the 1990s and the early years of the new century. Within a few years, ADHD went from being a much-discussed problem that the majority of Irish psychiatrists refused to diagnose to being the disorder most often diagnosed in children and adolescents referred to the mental health services. For Ireland's educational and mental health services, ADHD evolved from being a problem associated with poor parenting to become a complex, multidimensional disorder affecting the brain (Edwards & O'Donovan, 2018). Crucial aspects of the ADHD support organizations' role in promoting these changes were their alliance with experts who shared the same view of the disorder and their reliance on scientific evidence (Rabeharisoa, Moreira, & Akrich, 2014). Another important feature of their activism was their insistence on a multimodal approach to treating ADHD, which makes it necessary to go beyond the experience of any single professional.

After winning the battle to have ADHD in childhood acknowledged, the organizations then had to deal with the waiting lists for publicly financed mental health services. Other more recent battles and changes concern the acknowledgement of ADHD in adults too, and the consequent redefinition of the disorder. Irish activism in this area will probably contribute not only to an expansion of the boundaries of ADHD, but also to a growth in the number of the various "experts" (psychologists, psychiatrists, pharmacologists and neuroscientists, to mention just a few) engaging in research to find solutions for some of the problems posed by ADHD, and to meet the new demand for professional intervention.

Germany

The first descriptions of children who were hyperactive or inattentive in Germany date back a very long way, to the stories about *Zappelphilipp* (Fidgety Philip, a boy who was incapable of sitting still, even for a minute, from the moment he woke up until dinnertime) and *Hans Guck-in-die-Luft* (Johnny Head-in-the-Air, a dreamer who always seemed to live inside his own head) (Hoffmann, 1995). Nowadays, it is clear that these stories give an account of children with neurobiological problems that have cognitive and behavioural consequences, but at the time of their publication they were quoted as examples of the violation of social norms. It has taken many years for these characters to be seen as having an organic dysfunction rather than as examples of bad behaviour.

Judging from various studies conducted on children from 3 to 17 years old, the prevalence of this disorder in Germany today is around 5%, or 4% if we consider the ICD-10 diagnostic criteria (Grobe, Dörning, & Schwartz, 2013; Lange et al., 2014).

Official guidelines for ADHD developed and published by the *Deutsche Gesellschaft für Kinder- und Jugendpsychiatrie* (DGKJP, 2007) refer both to the ICD-10 and to the DSM-IV. They also indicate possible comorbidities, and they recommend a multimodal intervention. The guidelines describe the various types of treatment available, from counselling to the more recently introduced biofeedback. A combination of cognitive-behavioural therapies and pharmacological treatment is proposed as the gold standard (Deutsche Gesellschaft für Kinder-, Jugendpsychiatrie, Psychosomatik, & Psychotherapie, 2007). These guidelines are now considered obsolete and the DGKJP is working together with the *Deutsche Gesellschaft für Psychiatrie und Psychotherapie, Psychomatik und Nervenheilkunde* on the preparation of more up-to-date recommendations.

In Germany, as in the countries discussed previously, there has been lively debate on the issue of pharmacological treatments for ADHD. After initially campaigning against the use of medication (Conrad, 1983), groups of people with ADHD, parents of children with the disorder and other members of their families have begun to promote a better understanding of ADHD in Germany, also joining forces in self-help groups and associations. These groups have led to the creation of two important associations that, following various debates, have produced an informative booklet (*Bundeszentrale für gesundheitliche Aufklärung*, 2004), which describes the biomedical model of ADHD and the potential benefits of pharmacological treatment and self-help groups.

The current debate on ADHD in Germany shows that patients ardently want their condition to be acknowledged, and they are battling for easier access to pharmacological therapies. Although the biomedical approach to ADHD is still ambiguous and controversial, the use of drugs (usually methylphenidate) is considered an integral part of symptom management. In the world of ADHD, the boundaries between health and illness, and between symptom treatment and cognitive enhancement seem to be increasingly hazy. While the debate on neural enhancement (i.e. the use of drugs to improve cognitive performance) was dominated for a long time by critics of this approach, the use of drugs has recently become increasingly widespread in Germany. There has been a shift towards a greater variety of opinions, sometimes distinctly in favour of using medical treatment methods. In 2008, a statement from a group of illustrious authors and scientists that appeared in the British journal *Nature* (Greely et al., 2008) supported the idea that mature, responsible consumers should be allowed to acquire certain brain-enhancing drugs used to treat some neural disorders. If taken by healthy people, these drugs have the effect of improving cognitive performance for a more or less lengthy period of time. In Germany in 2009, a group of ethicists and scientists took a similar stance, publishing a statement of consent to promote discussion on a medical approach to cognitive enhancement (Galert et al., 2009). This change of heart may be due to the extremely limited availability of opportunities for neural enhancement interventions (Karsch, 2011).

Italy

By comparison with the previously mentioned countries, ADHD is a relatively new topic in Italy. Until the 1990s and even in the early years of this century, the condition was still not acknowledged by many psychiatrists and psychologists, and it was practically unknown to most of the general population (Conrad & Bergey, 2014). A study conducted in the mid-1980s (O'Leary, Vivian, & Cornoldi, 1984) investigated how psychiatrists and psychologists assessed the typical symptoms of ADHD in the United States and Italy. It emerged that Italian psychologists attributed these traits mainly to learning disorders or personality disorders. A study in 2001 showed that 60% of paediatricians were aware that ADHD existed, but did not know the criteria for its diagnosis, and only 10% of them followed up children with the disorder directly (Bonati, Impacciatore, & Pandolfini, 2001). In 2002, the Italian pharmaceuticals agency (*Agenzia Italiana del Farmaco*) approved the use of methylphenidate as a therapeutic option for children over six years old. Ritalin and Strattera became available in 2007 (Panei et al., 2004), the same year that a national drugs register was set up to collect and monitor diagnostic data on people receiving pharmacological treatments (Frazzetto, Keenan, & Singh, 2007).

Times have rapidly changed, however, and ADHD is now a diagnosis acknowledged by all professionals and known to the population at large. The activities of various organizations like the *Associazione Italiana Disturbi di Attenzione e Iperattività* (AIDAI) and the *Associazione Italiana Famiglie ADHD* (AIFA) have been important in driving the acceptance and recognition of ADHD. The AIDAI consists of professionals concerned with managing the disorder, while the AIFA helps the families of children who suffer from it. These associations have enabled the diffusion of an appropriate understanding of ADHD, and promoted legislation and social policies in favour of those affected. They have enabled teachers to receive appropriate training and supported the use of pharmacological treatments, where necessary. In contrast, other associations (such as *Giù le mani dai bambini*) have questioned the very existence of this type of disorder and the use of such pharmacological treatments, and launched the accusation that many types of human behaviour and human difficulties are being "pathologized".

An important national conference on ADHD held in 2003 (*Istituto Superiore di Sanità*, ISS, 2003) led to a consensus statement signed by the main clinical and scientific experts on the subject. This consensus statement promoted the concept of ADHD as a chronic neurodevelopmental disorder and provided specific directives on its diagnosis and cognitive-behavioural treatment in line with the DSM-IV-TR (APA, 2000). Reference was also made to the use of pharmacological treatment in the event of other psycho-educational intervention proving ineffectual. When the *Agenzia Italiana del Farmaco* (2007) approved the use of the psychoactive drug methylphenidate as the first choice for the pharmacological treatment of ADHD, and atomoxetine as a second choice (Germinario et al., 2013), the debate became even more lively and the criticism louder. In short, although the story of ADHD in Italy has been characterized by controversies, the country now takes a stance similar to that of the English-speaking countries in terms of its scientific knowledge of ADHD and its attention to its diagnosis and treatment, and more work is still being done to move further in this direction.

As regards the prevalence of ADHD in Italy, the latest study estimated it at 3% of the population from 5 to 15 years old (Bianchini et al., 2013), while no studies have been conducted on the adult population as yet. Among all cases of ADHD in 5- to 17-year-olds identified between 2007 and 2010, as many as 88.6% were male (Ruggiero et al., 2012).

In accordance with the national protocol (ISS, 2007), treatment for ADHD can be of three types: psychological-behavioural, pharmacological or multimodal (a combination of the other two). The first includes cognitive-behavioural intervention with the child, parent training and teacher training (or consulting services for teachers). Italy's national health service usually has lengthy waiting times, so families frequently turn to private clinics specializing in ADHD. For the time being, there are no services available for adults, however.

To establish a diagnosis, it is necessary to involve the family and the school, as well as the child, who is assessed in an interview and administered several tests.

At school, pupils with ADHD are included in normal classes like all other children (Italy has an inclusive schooling system). The current rules (MIUR, 2012) allow for tailored teaching plans to be adopted for students with ADHD to respond to their particular needs, and to offer them strategies and tools to optimize their learning experience.

France

France is one of the last European countries to address the topic of ADHD. By comparison with the other countries considered so far, it has continued to show a tendency to pay little academic attention to the disorder, and this probably helps to explain its late appearance on the public stage too. ADHD has emerged as a problem of interest to the public as a result of three things happening.

First of all, at the INSERM (*Institut National de la Santé et de la Recherche Medicale*), groups of experts on mental disorders, conduct disorders and learning disorders, including ADHD (which emerged as an unsolved condition), supplied the international bodies with a large body of literature, largely relating to the neurological field. This led to them taking a biological approach to these disorders, opening up a debate on their very nature. Such an approach, and the discussions that revolved around the topic in a highly conflictual atmosphere, somehow left the French psychodynamic trend out of the picture (Haute Autorité de Santé, 2014).

Second, working groups on ADHD were set up that have joined forces to keep the debate alive over the last 15 years. Their continuing efforts have helped to ensure a constant writing and rewriting of public policies concerning this condition (Edwards, Howlett, Akrich, & Rabeharisoa, 2014).

Third, the main group defending French patients with ADHD and their families, HyperSupers (established in 2002), undertook to mobilize scientists and clinicians with an interest in ADHD. Their efforts culminated in an international conference that the association organized jointly with ADHD Europa in 2009 (HyperSupers TDAH France, Vergnaud-Gétin, 2010). HyperSupers also conducted surveys and produced data on the experiences of families that have children with ADHD, which they presented to various groups of experts. As a result of their efforts on several fronts, the term TDAH (*Trouble Déficit de l'Attention/Hyperactivité*) was finally adopted and is now used by French specialists on ADHD.

The latest epidemiological study (Lecendreux, Konofal, & Faraone, 2011) set the prevalence of the disorder in France in the range of 3.5% to 5.6% of the paediatric population.

In 2005, INSERM described ADHD as an unsolved condition, placing it alongside mental disorders, conduct disorders and learning disorders in the category of "neurodevelopmental disorders", as in the DSM-5 (American Psychiatric Association, 2013).

Approaches to the treatment of ADHD have not been characterized by such a wholly neurological perspective, however. In fact, psychoanalysis has always been influential in France, and many psychiatrists have taken an "eclectic approach" that has prompted some of them to develop treatment models for ADHD that combine a variety of interventions (Vallée, 2011).

This overview of how ADHD has been dealt with in France in the last 15 years prompts two final considerations. Instead of ending the debate and limiting the further exploration of this disorder, the medicalization of ADHD has raised concerns and made various actors more aware of a variety of previously ignored problems – and coping with such a variety of issues is by no means easy. The second consideration concerns the fact that, by multiplying efforts to singularize ADHD and the associated disorders, specialists and other interested parties are coming up against the complex biological, psychological and social facets of these pathological conditions. Some important progress has nonetheless been made in France. Suffice it to mention that, at the end of the 1990s, the French still considered ADHD an American invention, whereas it is now recognized as a genuine disorder, even though it is still shrouded in controversy. But interventions for ADHD are bound to become a primary concern in France soon (Akrich & Rabeharisoa, 2018).

Argentina

In Argentina the pharmacological treatment of ADHD in children, based on the use of methylphenidate, has been a continual cause of lively debate. The picture that has emerged is extremely complex and involves professionals from fields as far apart as health, education, economics and politics. ADHD has become a place where all these fields and their respective actors meet, but unfortunately rarely cooperate. On the topic of ADHD in Argentina, there are three aspects that it seems important to mention.

First of all, state policy focusing on children's rights – particularly the *Ley Nacional de Salud Mental* (*Informacion Legislativa*, 2010), which is concerned with human rights, and the United Nations Convention on the Rights of the Child (OHCHR, 1990) – adopts a stance that refuses to pathologize childhood and opposes the pharmacological treatment of ADHD. This attitude is associated with another factor relating to clinical and therapeutic perspectives on psychoanalysis and various professional associations that tend to oppose advances made by the pharmaceutical industry and the DSM classification.

Another aspect of the situation in Argentina concerns the high costs of methylphenidate and other psychoactive pharmacological treatments that, combined with their exclusion from health cover plans, make them accessible only for the treatment of children of at least middle-class families.

The third aspect to mention concerns the legislation and rules governing the sale of psychoactive drugs for use in children (Argentina Pharmaceutical Country Profile, 2010). Their use for ADHD is still being resisted in Argentina, although pharmaceutical companies are conducting marketing campaigns to improve awareness and reach users, their families and the associations concerned with ADHD.

Brazil

The situation in Brazil is characterized by plenty of debate on the topic of ADHD. On one side, we see a vigorous group of physicians, psychiatrists and psychologists, among others, who are convinced that the condition is under-diagnosed and that public opinion, schools and parents should be better informed on the topic (Mattos, Rohde, & Polanczyk, 2012). On the other side, there are physicians and professionals in the human sciences who are constantly warning about society's limited tolerance of the ways children can typically behave, and its determination to find an easy way to manage them. Despite the medical disclosure of scientific information on ADHD (and supporting a diagnosis of ADHD, where applicable), it is impossible to ignore the polarization of the two above-described stances and the power of their contrasting claims. This is the picture that emerges from the literature, in journals published by professional associations and in open letters explaining the stances of one group or another, though their position statements are not always very explicit.

Leaving aside these controversies, it is worth noting that cases of ADHD in Brazil are diagnosed according to the ICD-10, while the DSM is only used for research purposes. There are no unequivocal data available on the prevalence of ADHD in Brazil as there is too much variability in the reported figures, which range between 3.6% and 17% of the paediatric population, depending on the methods used in the studies (Barbosa & Gouveia, 1993; Vasconcelos et al., 2003). As for treatments, we find that pharmacological therapies are promoted exclusively by the medical world. They seem to be used by about 18% of the individuals diagnosed (Mattos et al., 2012), almost always in combination with psychosocial treatments, including behavioural therapy and lifestyle changes, that are usually proposed by psychologists, teachers or educators.

Chile

In all the countries previously discussed, what emerges is the abundance of debate and the controversies, mainly focusing on pharmacological treatments for ADHD. That said, the situation that has persisted in Chile is rather different. Chile does not have its own story on ADHD. Knowledge of the disorder arrived from the United States and thanks to the contribution of an Argentinian psychiatrist. Methylphenidate was already marketed in Chile in 1960, but was only accepted by health professionals in the 1980s, ultimately becoming widespread in the 1990s (Jaque & Rodriguez, 2011). The crucial issue, however, is that it was used not only for children with a diagnosis of ADHD, but also for treating all those children who were difficult, strange or hard to manage. This is happening less nowadays, but the number of children diagnosed with ADHD is still very high. Problems of inattention and hyperactivity are the principal reasons for accessing the mental health services for children and adolescents, and even for adults (Vicente, Saldivia, Melipillán, Valdivia, & Kohn, 2012).

There are no official records, however, so it is impossible to know the prevalence of the disorder, or how many individuals diagnosed with ADHD are treated pharmacologically.

The increasingly widespread prescription and consumption of psychoactive drugs in Chile, and the growing debate on the so-called abuse of the diagnosis of ADHD are of interest, partly because these issues go to show how a psychiatric diagnosis that aims to apply "globally" can also be extremely contextual and local in its implementation. Education policies and an extremely strong neoliberal economy seem to be driving a constant, acute surveillance over children's actions and behaviour. This has led to a widespread use of methylphenidate as the quickest and easiest way to deal with the symptoms of ADHD. But, as we have emphasized several times before, there is a fairly widespread consensus that psychoactive drugs are only one dimension of the treatment of this disorder, and should be used in the short term in combination with other, nonpharmacological interventions. This does not seem to be what happens in daily practice, however (Céspedes, 2012; Rojas Flores, 2010).

In 2009 the *Ministerio de Educación* published a booklet with guidance on ADHD and suggested strategies for supporting children with the disorder. This is the only document on ADHD that contains official guidelines to help teachers and educators manage children with ADHD adequately. The guidelines emphasize the importance of working on the class setting, on the children's relationship with classmates and teachers, and on fully developing the abilities of students with special educational needs. Despite these guidelines, and the fact that Chile is one of the countries with the highest prevalence of children with ADHD (De la Barra, Vicente, Saldivia, & Melipillan, 2013), the Chilean government does not seem to have succeeded in developing an official programme for addressing the real impact and extent of the disorder and its possible treatment. For now, we can only hope that the promise of future interventions and studies will become a reality, generating a body of papers that will shed light on the situation of children and adolescents in Chile, while also acknowledging the shades of meaning applicable to the local context and social dynamics (Rojas Navarro, Rojas, & Peña Ochoa, 2018).

Japan

Research on ADHD has been very prolific in Japan, and has a lengthy history. At the start of the 20th century, the father of psychology, Yuzero Motora, developed a theory on inattention, describing symptoms similar to those of ADHD (Takeda, Ando, & Kumagai, 2015). The current prevalence of the disorder in Japan is between 3% and 7% of the paediatric population, in line with international research (Citizens Commission on Human

Rights, CCHR, 2018). The symptoms of the disorder must be present before seven years of age in order to establish the diagnosis, and no treatment can be administered before a child is six years old. A crucial aspect of Japan's approach to ADHD lies in that it is not acknowledged over 18 years of age, so there are no clinical indications for the treatment of the disorder in adults.

Another particular feature of how ADHD is seen in Japan concerns the fact that it comes under the umbrella term *hattatsu shogai*, which can be literally translated as "neurodevelopmental disorders" (a term adopted before it was used in the DSM-5 classification), along with autistic spectrum disorders and severe learning disorders. Grouping these problems together led to the disorders being heavily stigmatized, as some of their characteristics clash with Japanese educational and moral principles. This situation was exacerbated by a news story about a young boy who had brutally killed one of his peers when it subsequently became known that he had been diagnosed with ADHD. The pharmacological treatment of ADHD makes the stigma even worse in a country such as Japan, where all amphetamine-like stimulants are controlled in the same way as recreational narcotics. Although the Ministry of Health, Labour and Welfare recommends pharmacological therapy as part of the treatment of choice for ADHD, it is sometimes difficult to implement. Only two drugs are indicated as suitable for prescribing in this setting: Strattera, which is not psychoactive; and Concerta, which is psychoactive but with a long half-life (Okumura et al., 2019). The parents of children with ADHD generally prefer other types of treatment, possibly because of the associated stigma and Japanese culture: only 23% mention pharmacological treatment as being among the interventions they expect to be offered (Saito, 2005). The other types of treatment used for ADHD in Japan include parent training, "environmental coordination" and psychosocial intervention with the child. Environmental coordination involves adjusting the learning environment in the class and at home in order to manage the symptoms of ADHD more effectively (CCHR, 2018).

Taiwan

In Taiwan, ADHD is among the mental disorders of childhood and adolescence most often diagnosed in the last decade. The estimated prevalence among children between 7 and 15 years old is in the range 6.3–12% (Huang, 2008), higher than the 5% estimated around the world (Polanczyk, De Lima, Horta, Biederman, & Rohde, 2007). The procedures routinely used to diagnose and treat ADHD seem to refer to the latest knowledge and methods coming from abroad. But Taiwan's specialists in developmental psychiatry have not just unthinkingly imported psychiatric know-how and techniques from elsewhere. They have continued to consider the local setting, and always shared the "problem" and the "task" of these children's behaviour and learning with parents and teachers. This has given rise to an expanding network of expertise for managing "problematic children" with increasing numbers of social sectors involved.

Since the second half of the 1990s, Taiwan's national health insurance system (NHI) has become an infrastructure that manages almost all of the medical sector. The role of psychiatrists in this network has begun to weaken, as the NHI has developed a single payment system that restricts the autonomy of physicians. The work of other professionals, including clinical psychologists, social support workers and psychiatrists, is subject to a financial reimbursement scheme covering their services. Although many developmental psychiatrists are still trying to provide a more complete form of care for children with ADHD despite the NHI's unfavourable reimbursement system, the reconfiguration of the network is gradually eroding the bio-psychosocial approach to understanding and treating mental disorders in children. These changes are also undermining the multidisciplinary teamwork of the holistic public health system (Tseng, 2018).

The use of pharmacological therapies in Taiwan is supported mainly by teachers, whereas 38% of parents reject them (Hsu & Chan, 2008). Some parents refuse because of the side effects, others because they consider it more useful to the teachers who have to manage large classes, and some see it as an unacceptable way of labelling their children. Such thinking finds support among physicians of traditional Chinese medicine, who envisage a different aetiology for ADHD and rely on herbal formulas and acupuncture for its treatment, and it is also supported by some family doctors, who have spoken out against excesses in the diagnosis and treatment of hyperactive children (Yu, Huang, & Yen, 2011).

Ghana

In Ghana a handful of physicians, mainly trained abroad, adopt the diagnosis of ADHD based on the DSM and treat this condition with various drugs (haloperidol, chlorpromazine, carbamazepine, imipramine, atomoxetine or methylphenidate), depending on availability.

ADHD support associations linked with those of Western countries and a pharmaceutical company have recently tried to improve the general public's awareness of the disorder (Kleintjes, Lund, & Flisher, 2010). Government guidelines included ADHD in 2010, but there is still virtually no standardized diagnostic procedure or treatment for the disorder. The lack of its institutional acknowledgement and the country's limited resources mean that ADHD is still not a well-known diagnostic category. Physicians may establish a diagnosis for children who are sent to them by parents and teachers, though psychiatrists, clinical psychologists and paediatricians are usually the last resort, after healers and priests have been consulted in vain (Read & Doku, 2013; Snyman & Truter, 2010).

An exploratory study among clinicians found that ADHD in Ghana poses a problem of respect for older people. Being steeped in cultural values in which reciprocity and respect are key concepts, any undisciplined behaviour at school is seen mainly as a demonstration of disobedience towards the teachers and indifference to punishment (Twum-Danso, 2009).

Stubborn and *disobedient* are the terms most likely to be used in Ghana to describe a child who is not listening, not paying attention, speaking too loudly in an adult's presence, being restless and especially not showing humility. Being stubborn and disobedient is unacceptable behaviour because it is assumed to stem from a lack of respect.

As in the West, in Ghana school classrooms are among the main places where the problems of children with ADHD become manifest, and their academic performance suffers. For a child to do well at school is seen as a sign of respect and obedience. Failing academically and leaving school early are associated not just with a problem of skills, but also with an inability or unwillingness to obey the rules (McIntyre & Hennessy, 2010; Seabi & Economou, 2012).

Training clinicians (often abroad), importing pharmaceutical products and the work of NGOs serve as the means to improve the diagnosis and treatment of ADHD in Ghana. Given its lack of institutional acknowledgement and the stigma associated with the diagnosis of a mental disorder, it is hard to say whether ADHD may eventually become a way of dealing with the problems of Ghanaian children who are inattentive and/or hyperactive. Meanwhile, the situation in Ghana suggests that the diffusion of ADHD in the country is still not as evident as in the majority of Western countries, or as strongly influenced by the latter's dominant, medicalizing approach (Bröer, Spronk, & Kraak, 2018).

What emerges clearly from our travels around the world is that, although the meaning of ADHD has become more global and shared in recent years – sometimes thanks to research and the work of experts, sometimes thanks to patients and their families – it is still a concept that depends on where the disorder is diagnosed. Location also influences how it is treated, and the stigma attached to it.

Despite scientific progress bringing various benefits in terms of the treatment of ADHD, we need to continue to reflect on the meaning of its symptoms and the psychological, social and relational problems it poses.

References

Akrich, M., & Rabeharisoa, V. (2018). The French ADHD landscape: Maintaining and dealing with multiple uncertainties. In M. R. Bergey, M. Filipe, P. Conrad, & I. Singh (Eds.), *Global perspectives on ADHD: Social dimensions of diagnosis and treatment in sixteen countries* (pp. 233–260). Baltimore, MD: Johns Hopkins University Press.

Al-Yagon, M., Cavendish, W., Cornoldi, C., Fawcett, A. J., Grünke, M., Hung, L. Y., & Margalit, M. (2013). The proposed changes for DSM-5 for SLD and ADHD: International perspectives – Australia, Germany, Greece, India, Israel, Italy, Spain, Taiwan, United Kingdom, and United States. *Journal of Learning Disabilities, 46*(1), 58–72.

American Academy of Paediatrics. (2011). ADHD: Clinical practice guideline for diagnosis, evaluation, and treatment of attention-deficit/hyperactivity disorder in children and adolescents. *Pediatrics, 128*, 1007–1022.

American Psychiatric Association. (2000). *Diagnostic and statistical manual of mental disorders* (4th Ed Revised ed.), ((DSM-IV-TR)). Washington DC: Author.

American Psychiatric Association. (2013). *Diagnostic and statistical manual of mental disorders* (5th ed.). Washington, DC: Author.

Barbosa, G. A., & Gouveia, V. V. (1993). O fator hiperatividade do Questionário de Conners: validação conceptual e normas diagnósticas [The hyperactivity factor of the Conners Questionnaire: conceptual validation and diagnostic norms]. *Temas: Teoria e Prática do Psiquiatra, 23*(46), 188–202.

Bergey, M. R. (2015). *The rise of attention deficit hyperactivity disorder (ADHD) coaching: The social meanings and policy implications of a new approach for managing ADHD* (Doctoral dissertation). Brandeis University, Waltham, Massachusetts, United States.

Bergey, M. R., Filipe, A. M., Conrad, P., & Singh, I. (Eds.). (2018). *Global perspectives on ADHD: Social dimensions of diagnosis and treatment in sixteen countries*. Baltimore, MD: Johns Hopkins University Press.

Bianchini, R., Postorino, V., Grasso, R., Santoro, B., Migliore, S., Burlò, C., … Mazzone, L. (2013). Prevalence of ADHD in a sample of Italian students: A population-based study. *Research in Developmental Disabilities, 34*(9), 2543–2550.

Bloom, B., Jones, L. I., & Freeman, G. (2013). Summary health statistics for US children: National health interview survey, 2012. *Vital and Health Statistics, 10*(258), 1–81.

Blum, L. M. (2015). *Raising generation Rx: Mothering kids with invisible disabilities in an age of inequality*. New York, NY: NYU Press.

Bonati, M., Impacciatore, P., & Pandolfini, C. (2001). Evidence and belief in attention deficit hyperactivity disorder: Reintroduction of methylphenidate in Italy needs careful monitoring. *British Medical Journal, 322*, 556.

Bröer, C., Spronk, R., & Kraak, V. (2018). Exploring the ADHD diagnosis in Ghana: Between disrespect and lack of institutionalization. In M. R. Bergey, M. Filipe, P. Conrad, & I. Singh (Eds.), *Global perspectives on ADHD: Social dimensions of diagnosis and treatment in sixteen countries* (pp. 354–375). Baltimore, MD: Johns Hopkins University Press.

Bundesinstitut für gesundheitliche Aufklärung. (2004). *ADHS. Aufmerksamkeitsdefizit/hyperaktivitätsstörung … was bedeutet das? [ADHD. Attention deficit/hyperactivity disorder … what does that mean?]*. Köln: Selbstverlag Bachem.

Canadian Attention Deficit Hyperactivity Disorder Resource Alliance (CADDRA). (2011). *Canadian ADHD practice guidelines,3*.

Céspedes, A. (2012). *Déficit Atencional en niños y adolescents [Attention deficit in children and adolescents]*. Santiago de Chile: Ediciones B Chile.

Charach, A., Lin, E., & To, T. (2010). Evaluating the hyperactivity/inattention subscale of the national longitudinal survey of children and youth. *Health Reports, 21*(2), 45.

Citizens Commission on Human Rights. (2018). ADHD labelling and treatment of children in Japan. *CCHR Reports*, 1–12.

Conrad, P. (1983). Die Entdeckung der Hyperkinese. Anmerkungen zur Medizinisierung abweichenden Verhaltens [The discovery of hyperkinesis: Comments on mediating deviant behavior]. *Pillen für den Störenfried*, 93–104.

Conrad, P., & Bergey, M. R. (2014). The impending globalization of ADHD: Notes on the expansion and growth of a medicalized disorder. *Social Science & Medicine, 122*, 31–43.

Conrad, P., & Potter, D. (2000). From hyperactive children to ADHD adults: Observations on the expansion of medical categories. *Social Problems, 47*(4), 559–582.

De la Barra, F. E., Vicente, B., Saldivia, S., & Melipillan, R. (2013). Epidemiology of ADHD in Chilean children and adolescents. *ADHD Attention Deficit and Hyperactivity Disorders, 5*(1), 1–8.

Deutsche Gesellschaft für Kinder-, Jugendpsychiatrie, Psychosomatik, & Psychotherapie. (2007). *Leitlinien zu Diagnostik und Therapie von psychischen Störungen im Säuglings-, Kindes-und Jugendalter [Guidelines on diagnosis and treatment of mental disorders in infants, children and adolescents]*. Köln: Deutscher Ärzte Verlag.

Edmunds, A., & Martsch-Litt, S. (2008). ADHD assessment and diagnosis in Canada: An inconsistent but fixable process. *Exceptionality Education International, 18*(2), 2–23.

Edwards, C., Howlett, E., Akrich, M., & Rabeharisoa, V. (2014). Attention deficit hyperactivity disorder in France and Ireland: Parents' groups' scientific and political framing of an unsettled condition. *BioSocieties, 9*(2), 153–172.

Edwards, C., & O'Donovan, Ó. (2018). Transformations in the Irish ADHD disorder regime: From a disorder "you have to fight to get" to one "you have to wait to get". In M. R. Bergey, M. Filipe, P. Conrad, & I. Singh (Eds.), *Global perspectives on ADHD: Social dimensions of diagnosis and treatment in sixteen countries* (pp. 138–161). Baltimore, MD: Johns Hopkins University Press.

Frazzetto, G., Keenan, S., & Singh, I. (2007). 'I Bambini e le Droghe': The right to Ritalin vs the right to childhood in Italy. *BioSocieties, 2*(4), 393–412.

Galert, T., Bublitz, C., Heuser, I., Merkel, R., Repantis, D., Schöne-Seifert, B., & Talbot, D. (2009). Das optimierte Gehirn. Ein memorandum zu chencen und risiken des neuroenhancements [The optimized brain. To memorandum and risks of neuroenhancements]. *Gehirn und Geist, 11*, 40–48.

Germinario, E. A., Arcieri, R., Bonati, M., Zuddas, A., Masi, G., & Vella, S. Panei, and the Italian ADHD Regional Reference Centres, P. (2013). Attention-deficit/hyperactivity disorder drugs and growth: An Italian prospective observational study. *Journal of Child and Adolescent Psychopharmacology, 23*(7), 440–447.

Greely, H., Sahakian, B., Harris, J., Kessler, R. C., Gazzaniga, M., Campbell, P., & Farah, M. J. (2008). Towards responsible use of cognitive-enhancing drugs by the healthy. *Nature, 456*(7223), 702.

Grobe, T. G., Dörning, H., & Schwartz, F. W. (2013). Barmer GEK Arztreport 2013 [Barmer GEK Physician Report 2013]. *Schriftreihe zur Gesundheitsanalyse, 18,* 160–173.

Hoffmann, H. (1995). *Struwwelpeter.* Chelmsford, MA: Courier Corporation.

Hsu, C. C., & Chan, S. Y. (2008). A survey study on aspects of elementary school teachers toward students with different disabilities in regular classes. *Bulletin of Special Education and Rehabilitation, 19,* 25–49.

Huang, H. L. (2008). Review of attention deficit hyperactivity disorder (ADHD) research in Taiwan. *Research in Applied Psychology, 40,* 197–219.

Istituto Superiore di Sanità (2003). Conferenza nazionale di consenso: indicazioni e strategie terapeutiche per i bambini e gli adolescenti con disturbo da deficit attentivo e iperattività [National consensus conference: indications and therapeutic strategies for children and adolescents with attention deficit disorder and hyperactivity]. Cagliari 6–7 marzo 2003.

Jaque, J., & Rodriguez, F. L. (2011) Los veintes años de la generación Ritalín. *La Tercera, Santiago,* 4–5.

Karsch, F. (2011). Neuro-Enhancement oder Krankheitsbehandlung? Zur Problematik der Entgrenzung von Krankheit und Gesundheit am Beispiel ADHS [Neuro-enhancement or disease treatment? On the problem of the demarcation of disease and health using the example of ADHD]. *Entgrenzung der Medizin. Von der Heilkunst zur Verbesserung des Menschen,* 121–142.

Kleintjes, S., Lund, C., & Flisher, A. J. (2010). A situational analysis of child and adolescent mental health services in Ghana, Uganda, South Africa and Zambia. *African Journal of Psychiatry, 13,* 2.

Lange, M., Butschalowsky, H. G., Jentsch, F., Kuhnert, R., Rosario, A. S., & Schlaud, M. KiGGS Study Group. (2014). Die erste KiGGS-Folgebefragung [The first KiGGS follow-up survey]. *Bundesgesundheitsblatt-Gesundheitsforschung-Gesundheitsschutz, 57*(7), 747–761.

Lecendreux, M., Konofal, E., & Faraone, S. V. (2011). Prevalence of attention deficit hyperactivity disorder and associated features among children in France. *Journal of Attention Disorders, 15*(6), 516–524.

Malacrida, C. (2004). Medicalization, ambivalence and social control: Mothers' descriptions of educators and ADD/ADHD. *Health, 8*(1), 61–80.

Malacrida, C., & Semach, T. (2018). In the elephant's shadow. In M. R. Bergey, M. Filipe, P. Conrad, & I. Singh (Eds.), *Global perspectives on ADHD: Social dimensions of diagnosis and treatment in sixteen countries* (pp. 34–53). Baltimore, MD: Johns Hopkins University Press.

Mattos, P., Rohde, L. A. P., & Polanczyk, G. V. (2012). ADHD is undertreated in Brazil. *Revista brasileira de psiquiatria, 34*(4), 513–514.

McCabe, S. E. (2008). Misperceptions of non-medical prescription drug use: A web survey of college students. *Addictive Behaviors, 33*(5), 713–724.

McIntyre, R., & Hennessy, E. (2010). He's just enthusiastic. Is that such a bad thing? Experiences of parents of children with attention deficit hyperactivity disorder. *Emotional and Behavioural Difficulties, 17*(1), 65–82.

MIUR (Ministero dell'Istruzione dell'Università e della Ricerca). (2012). Strumenti d'intervento per alunni con bisogni educativi speciali e organizzazione territoriale per l'inclusione scolastica [Intervention tools for pupils with special educational needs and territorial organization for school inclusion]. *Direttiva Ministeriale 27 dicembre 2012.*

Morgan, P. L., Staff, J., Hillemeier, M. M., Farkas, G., & Maczuga, S. (2013). Racial and ethnic disparities in ADHD diagnosis from kindergarten to eighth grade. *Pediatrics, 132*(1), 85–93.

Murphy, J. M., McCarthy, A. E., Baer, L., Zima, B. T., & Jellinek, M. S. (2014). Alternative national guidelines for treating attention and depression problems in children: Comparison of treatment approaches and prescribing rates in the United Kingdom and United States. *Harvard Review of Psychiatry, 22*(3), 179–192.

NHMRC (National Health and Medical Research Council). (1997). *Attention Deficit Hyperactivity Disorder.* Canberra: Australian Government Publishing Service.

NHMRC (National Health and Medical Research Council (Australia). (2012). *Clinical practice points on the diagnosis, assessment and management of attention deficit hyperactivity disorder in children and adolescents.* Australian Government, National Health and Medical Research Council.

Navarro, S. R., Rojas, P., & Ochoa, M. P. (2018). From problematic children to problematic diagnosis. In M. R. Bergey, M. Filipe, P. Conrad, & I. Singh (Eds.), *Global perspectives on ADHD: Social dimensions of diagnosis and treatment in sixteen countries* (pp. 310–331). Baltimore, MD: Johns Hopkins University Press.

O'Leary, K. D., Vivian, D., & Cornoldi, C. (1984). Assessment and treatment of "hyperactivity"; In Italy and the United States. *Journal of Clinical Child & Adolescent Psychology, 13*(1), 56–60.

Okumura, Y., Usami, M., Okada, T., Saito, T., Negoro, H., Tsujii, N., ... & Iida, J. (2019). Prevalence, incidence and persistence of ADHD drug use in Japan. *Epidemiology and psychiatric sciences, 28*(6), 692–696.

Panei, P., Arcieri, R., Vella, S., Bonati, M., Martini, N., & Zuddas, A. (2004). Italian attention-deficit/hyperactivity disorder registry. *Pediatrics*, *114*(2), 514.

Polanczyk, G., De Lima, M. S., Horta, B. L., Biederman, J., & Rohde, L. A. (2007). The worldwide prevalence of ADHD: A systematic review and metaregression analysis. *American Journal of Psychiatry*, *164*(6), 942–948.

Prosser, B. J., & Graham, L. J. (2018). Historical, cultural, and sociopolitical influences on Australia's response to ADHD. In *Global perspectives on ADHD: Social dimensions of diagnosis and treatment in sixteen countries* (p. 54). Baltimore, MD: Johns Hopkins University.

Rabeharisoa, V., Moreira, T., & Akrich, M. (2014). Evidence-based activism: Patients', users' and activists' groups in knowledge society. *BioSocieties*, *9*, 111–128.

Read, U. M., & Doku, V. (2013). Mental health research in Ghana: A literature review. *Ghana Medical Journal*, *46*(2), 29–38.

Reid, R., Maag, J. W., & Vasa, S. F. (1993). Attention deficit hyperactivity disorder as a disability category: A critique. *Exceptional Children*, *60*(3), 198–214.

Rojas Flores, J. (2010). Historia de la infancia en el Chile republicano, 1810-2010 [History of childhood in Republican Chile, 1810-2010]. *Santiago de Chile: Ocholibros*.

Ruggiero, S., Rafaniello, C., Bravaccio, C., Grimaldi, G., Granato, R., Pascotto, A., ... Rossi, F. (2012). Safety of attention-deficit/hyperactivity disorder medications in children: An intensive pharmaco surveillance monitoring study. *Journal of Child and Adolescent Psychopharmacology*, *22*(6), 415–422.

Saito, M. (2005). Diagnosis and therapeutic guideline for attention deficit hyperkinetic syndrome (ADHD). *Seishin shinkeigaku zasshi [Psychiatria et neurologia Japonica]*, *107*(2), 167–179.

Seabi, J., & Economou, N. A. (2012). Understanding the distracted and the disinhibited: Experiences of adolescents diagnosed with ADHD within the South African context. In M. Norvilities (Ed.)*Contemporary Trends in ADHD Research*, 165–182. Rijeka, HR: IntechOpen.

Singh, I. (2006). A framework for understanding trends in ADHD diagnoses and stimulant drug treatment: schools and schooling as a case study. *BioSocieties*, *1*(4), 439–452.

Singh, I. (2018). ADHD in the United Kingdom: Conduct, class and stigma. In M. R. Bergey, M. Filipe, P. Conrad, & I. Singh (Eds.), *Global perspectives on ADHD: Social dimensions of diagnosis and treatment in sixteen countries* (pp. 97–117). Baltimore, MD: Johns Hopkins University Press.

Singh, I., Filipe, A. M., Bard, I., Bergey, M., & Baker, L. (2013). Globalization and cognitive enhancement: Emerging social and ethical challenges for ADHD clinicians. *Current Psychiatry Reports, 15*(9), 385–397.

Snyman, S., & Truter, I. (2010). Complementary and alternative medicine for attention deficit/hyperactivity disorder: An Eastern Cape study. *South African Family Practice, 52*(2), 161–162.

Takeda, T., Ando, M., & Kumagai, K. (2015). Attention deficit and attention training in early twentieth-century Japan. *ADHD Attention Deficit and Hyperactivity Disorders, 7*(2), 101–111.

Timimi, S. (2008). Child psychiatry and its relationship with the pharmaceutical industry: Theoretical and practical issues. *Advances in Psychiatric Treatment, 14*(1), 3–9.

Tseng, F. T. (2018). The development of child psychiatry and the biomedicalization of ADHD in Taiwan. In M. R. Bergey, M. Filipe, P. Conrad, & I. Singh (Eds.), *Global perspectives on ADHD: Social dimensions of diagnosis and treatment in sixteen countries* (pp. 332–353). Baltimore, MD: Johns Hopkins University Press.

Twum-Danso, A. (2009). Reciprocity, respect and responsibilities: The 3Rs underlying parent–child relationships in Ghana and the implication for children's rights. *International Journal of Children's Rights, 17*(3), 415–432.

Vallée, M. (2011). Resisting American psychiatry: French opposition to DSM-III, biological reductionism, and the pharmaceutical ethos. In P. McGann & D. Hutson, (Eds.),*Sociology of diagnosis* (pp. 85–110). Bingley, UK: Emerald Group Publishing Limited.

Vasconcelos, M. M., Werner, J., Jr, Malheiros, A. F. D. A., Lima, D. F. N., Santos, Í. S. O., & Barbosa, J. B. (2003). Prevalência do transtorno de déficit de atenção/hiperatividade numa escola pública primária [Prevalence of attention deficit/hyperactivity disorder in a public elementary school]. *Arq Neuropsiquiatr, 61*(1), 67–73.

Vergnaud-Gétin, C. (2010). Aspects familiaux, association HyperSupers–TDAH France [Family aspects, association HyperSupers-ADHD France]. In O. Revol, & V. Brun (Eds),*Trouble Déficit De L'attention Avec Ou Sans Hyperactivité [Deficit disorder in attention with or without hyperactivity]* (pp. 30–35). Issy les Moulineaux, FR: Elsevier Masson.

Vicente, B., Saldivia, S., Melipillán, R., Valdivia, M., & Kohn, R. (2012). Prevalence of psychiatric disorders among Chilean children and adolescents. *Revista medica de Chile, 140*(4), 447–457.

Visser, S., Danielson, M. S. P. H., Bitsko, R., Holbrook, J. R., Kogan, M. D., Ghandour, R. M., ... Blumberg, S. J. (2014). Trends in the parent-report of health care provider-diagnosis and medication treatment for ADHD disorder: United States, 2003–2011. *Journal of the American Academy of Child & Adolescent Psychiatry, 53*(1), 34–46.

World Health Organization. (2010). ICD-10: International statistical classification of diseases and related health problems: Tenth revision (2nd ed.). Geneva, Switzerland: Author.

Yu, C. H., Huang, T. P., & Yen, H. R. (2011). The overview of attention deficit hyperactivity disorder in Chinese medicine and conventional medicine and its evidence base studies. *The Taipei Researches of Traditional Chinese Medical Journal*, 14(2), 79–93.

Zuvekas, S. H., & Vitiello, B. (2012). Stimulant medication use in children: A 12-year perspective. *American Journal of Psychiatry*, *169* (2), 160–166.

Website links

Agenzia Italiana del Farmaco (2007). https://www.gazzettaufficiale.it/eli/id/2007/04/24/07A03653/sg

Argentina Pharmaceutical Country Profile (2010). http://apps.who.int/medicinedocs/documents/s19736en/s19736en.pdf

Haute Autorité de Santé (2014). https://www.has-sante.fr/upload/docs/application/pdf/2015-02/tdah_argumentaire.pdf

IDEA (1991). https://sites.ed.gov/idea/about-idea/

Informacion Legislativa (2010). http://servicios.infoleg.gob.ar/infolegInternet/verNorma.do?id=175977

ISS (2007). http://old.iss.it/binary/adhd/cont/Protocollo%20diagnostico%20ADHD%20020507.1178184452.pdf

NHMRC (2012). https://www.nhmrc.gov.au/sites/default/files/images/clinical-practicepoints-diagnosis-assessment.pdf

NICE (2013). https://www.nice.org.uk/guidance/qs39

NSCH (2016). https://www.cdc.gov/ncbddd/adhd/data.html

OHCHR (1990). https://www.ohchr.org/en/professionalinterest/pages/crc.aspx

Index

Note: References in *italics* are to figures, those in **bold** to tables.

Taylor & Francis eBooks

www.taylorfrancis.com

A single destination for eBooks from Taylor & Francis
with increased functionality and an improved user
experience to meet the needs of our customers.

90,000+ eBooks of award-winning academic content in
Humanities, Social Science, Science, Technology, Engineering,
and Medical written by a global network of editors and authors.

TAYLOR & FRANCIS EBOOKS OFFERS:

A streamlined
experience for
our library
customers

A single point
of discovery
for all of our
eBook content

Improved
search and
discovery of
content at both
book and
chapter level

REQUEST A FREE TRIAL
support@taylorfrancis.com

For Product Safety Concerns and Information please contact our EU
representative GPSR@taylorandfrancis.com
Taylor & Francis Verlag GmbH, Kaufingerstraße 24, 80331 München, Germany

www.ingramcontent.com/pod-product-compliance
Lightning Source LLC
Chambersburg PA
CBHW050522280326
41932CB00014B/2415